ASHE-ERIC Higher Education Report: Volume 30, Number 2
Adrianna J. Kezar, Series Editor

Retaining Minority Students in Higher Education

A Framework for Success

Watson Scott Swail,
with Kenneth E. Redd and Laura W. Perna

Retaining Minority Students in Higher Education: A Framework for Success
Watson Scott Swail, with Kenneth E. Redd and Laura W. Perna
ASHE-ERIC Higher Education Report: Volume 30, Number 2
Adrianna J. Kezar, Series Editor

This publication was prepared partially with funding from the Office of Educational Research and Improvement, U.S. Department of Education, under contract no. ED-99-00-0036. The opinions expressed in this report do not necessarily reflect the positions or policies of OERI or the Department.

ISSN 0884-0040   electronic ISSN 1536-0709   ISBN 0-7879-7247-9

The ASHE-ERIC Higher Education Report is part of the Jossey-Bass Higher and Adult Education Series and is published six times a year by Wiley Subscription Services, Inc., A Wiley Company, at Jossey-Bass, 989 Market Street, San Francisco, California 94103-1741.

For subscription information, see the Back Issue/Subscription Order Form in the back of this journal.

CALL FOR PROPOSALS: Prospective authors are strongly encouraged to contact Adrianna Kezar at the University of Southern California, Waite Phillips Hall 703C, Los Angeles, CA 90089, or kezar@usc.edu. See "About the ASHE-ERIC Higher Education Report Series" in the back of this volume.

Visit the Jossey-Bass Web site at **www.josseybass.com.**

Printed in the United States of America on acid-free recycled paper.

Executive Summary

Today about half of students with dreams and aspirations based on their future receipt of an earned certificate or degree leave with that dream either stalled or ended. Access and completion rates for African American, Hispanic, and Native American students have always lagged behind white and Asian students, as have those for low-income students and students with disabilities. Although postsecondary enrollment rates for students of color are at levels similar to white and Asian students, access to four-year colleges, especially our nation's most selective institutions, remains inequitable. Beyond access, students of color have not earned degrees at the same rates as other students.

This ASHE-ERIC monograph is intended as a reference for key stakeholders regarding the realities of and strategies for student retention. It is our hope that it will serve as a "compass" for those with the complex task of improving retention.

Part One: Postsecondary Opportunity

Education has a profound impact on both the individual and society. Individuals with a bachelor's degree earn, on average, twice that of high school graduates, and those with a professional degree earn twice what individuals with a bachelor's earn. Thus, the demand for postsecondary education has increased greatly over the past several decades, with enrollments up ten-fold since the mid-1900s to approximately 14 million.

Educational attainment levels continue to be substantially lower for African Americans, Hispanics, and American Indians than for whites and Asians. In

2000, only 11 percent of Hispanics and 17 percent of blacks in the U.S. population age 25 and older had attained at least a bachelor's degree, compared with 28 percent of whites and 44 percent of Asians. A review of available data suggests that increasing the share of students of color who attain a bachelor's degree requires attention to four critical junctures.

Critical Juncture 1: Academic Preparation for College

Research shows that the level of academic preparation in high school is positively related to high school graduation rates, college entrance examination scores, predisposition toward college, college enrollment, representation at more selective colleges and universities, rates of transfer from a two-year to a four-year institution, progress toward earning a bachelor's degree by age 30, college persistence rates, and college completion rates. Completing a rigorous curricular program during high school appears to be a more important predictor of college persistence than test scores, particularly for African American and Hispanic students.

Critical Juncture 2: Graduation from High School

In 2000, 43 percent of Hispanics in the U.S. population age 25 and older had not completed high school, compared with 21 percent of blacks, 14 percent of Asians, and 12 percent of whites. These and other data suggest that one source of observed racial and ethnic group differences in educational attainment is lower rates of high school graduation, especially among Hispanic men and women.

Critical Juncture 3: Enrollment in College

Annual college enrollment rates have generally increased among high school graduates between the ages of 18 and 24 for blacks, Hispanics, and whites since the late 1980s. However, the share of black high school graduates enrolled in a degree-granting institution remained virtually unchanged between 1979 and 1989 but increased through the 1990s. Similarly, the shares of Hispanic high school graduates were comparable in 1979 and 1989 but higher in 1999. In contrast, the share of white high school graduates enrolled in college increased across both decades.

Critical Juncture 4: Persistence in College to Bachelor's Degree Completion

Only 46 percent of African Americans and 47 percent of Hispanics who first enrolled in a four-year institution in 1995–96 with the goal of completing a bachelor's degree actually completed a bachelor's degree within six years, compared to 67 percent of whites and 72 percent of Asians. Six-year bachelor's degree completion rates are also lower for African Americans and Hispanics than for whites and Asians at both types of institutions.

The Affirmative Action Debate

The recent decision by the U.S. Supreme Court allowing the University of Michigan to continue considering race as a factor in student admissions has once again brought affirmative action to the forefront of American higher education. However, while the Court's five-to-four ruling in *Grutter v. Bollinger* allows selective colleges and universities to continue using affirmative action plans to recruit and retain a "critical mass" of African American, Hispanic, and Native American students, it also urges college officials to prepare to dismantle racial diversity plans within twenty-five years (Lane, 2003). On the same day, the Supreme Court's ruling in *Gratz v. Bollinger* struck down the University of Michigan's undergraduate affirmative action admissions plan, which used a point system to rank prospective student applications. The two rulings mean that selective institutions are allowed to use affirmative action programs as long as institutions' admissions officers consider each prospective student's individual characteristics and academic records without using a point or ranking system. That is, race may be a "plus factor" in admissions decisions (Lane, 2003, p. A1). While the Supreme Court's decision has clarified the legality of affirmative action plans for colleges and universities, it has not ended the contentious debate on this issue.

Part Two: Why Students Leave College

Tinto's Student Integration Model (1975), based in part on Durkheim's theory of suicide, theorizes that the social integration of students increases their institutional commitment, ultimately reducing the likelihood of student attrition. Several researchers have used important aspects of Tinto's academic and social integration theory in the development of a psychological, rather than socio-logical, model. A number of researchers have found shortcomings in persistence and integration models. However, the complexity of the human condition makes it difficult to definitely prove the validity of one psychological or sociological theoretical model over another.

Factors Related to Retention

There are a number of factors related to retention, and researchers have found differences, as well as similarities, between white students and students of color.

Academic Preparedness. Research shows that between 30 and 40 percent of all entering freshmen are unprepared for college-level reading and writing and approximately 44 percent of all college students who complete a two- or four-year degree had enrolled in at least one remedial or developmental course in math, writing, or reading.

Campus Climate. While researchers agree that "institutional fit" and campus integration are important to retaining college students to degree completion, campus climate mediates undergraduates' academic and social experiences in college. Minority students inadequately prepared for non-academic challenges can experience culture shock. Lack of diversity in the student population, faculty, staff, and curriculum often restrict the nature and quality of minority students' interactions within and out of the classroom, threatening their academic performance and social experiences.

Commitment to Educational Goals and the Institution. The stronger the educational goal and institutional commitment, the more likely the student will graduate (Tinto, 1993). Research shows that congruence between student goals and institutional mission is mediated by academic and social components, and that increased integration into academic and social campus communities causes greater institutional commitment and student persistence.

Social and Academic Integration. The process of becoming socially integrated into the fabric of the university has also been found to be both a cumulative and compounding process, and the level of social integration within a given year of study is part of a cumulative experience that continues to build throughout one's college experience. The establishment of peer relations and the development of role models and mentors have been defined in the literature as important factors in student integration, both academically and socially.

Financial Aid. For many low-income and minority students, enrollment and persistence decisions are driven by the availability of financial aid. In 1999–2000, 77 percent of financially dependent students from families with less than $20,000 in family income received some financial aid, with an average award of $6,727. In contrast, 44 percent of those from families with income of $100,000 or more received aid, with an average award of $7,838.

Low-income and minority students who receive grants generally are more likely to persist than those who receive loans. However, given the rising costs of attending college, it is unlikely that low-income students will be able to receive bachelor's degrees without *any* loan aid. At the same time, the research also suggests that the shifts in aid from grants to loans and from need-based to merit-based programs adversely affects both enrollment and persistence for minority students. Reversing these shifts may be needed to increase college access and success for low-income and minority students.

Part Three: A Framework for Retention

While student persistence models remain useful in illustrating the problems and processes relating to student persistence, the relationship between college and student is lost between the simplicity and complexity of the various models. The Geometric Model of Student Persistence and Achievement provides a user-friendly method to discuss and focus on the cognitive and social attributes that the student brings to campus, plus the institutional role in the student experience. The geometric model also allows us to discuss the dynamics between cognitive, social, and institutional factors, all of which take place within the student. These three forces must combine to provide a solid foundation for student growth, development, and persistence.

This campus-wide retention model was designed to provide administrators with a strategy and framework to build a student retention plan that incorporates the individual needs of their students and institution. From an administrative perspective, the model's strategies are not prescriptive. They are alternatives and institutional practices that are consistent with both current thinking within the various communities and what we have been able to ascertain through the research literature. The retention framework is classified into five components based upon an extensive review of current literature: financial aid, recruitment and admissions, academic services, student services, and curriculum and instruction. The framework components are further broken down into categories based on areas of specialization, and subsequently into specific objectives.

Part Four: Implementation and Leadership

The development of any program at any university requires a multifaceted process incorporating all campus officials, including administration, faculty, staff, and especially students. Leadership and faculty ownership are key variables in a successful retention program, and the message communicated from top management is critical to the support of the campus staff.

To implement retention programs, senior campus leadership must play two important roles: monitoring institutional progress toward clearly stated campus retention goals, and coordinating and leading all stakeholders—students, parents, other campus administrators, faculty, and staff—toward stated goals. Through our discussions with stakeholders, as well as our review of related research, we were able to come up with a short list of essential factors in establishing such a program. A comprehensive student retention program must

- rely on proven research
- suit the particular needs of the campus
- be institutionalized and become a regular part of campus service
- involve all campus departments and all campus personnel
- take into consideration the dynamics of the change process and provide extensive and appropriate retraining of staff

- be student-centered
- operate in a cost-effective way, and not tied to soft monies
- have the support of a comprehensive student monitoring system that will become the foundation of all institutional research on campus and support every department
- be sensitive to student needs and to diverse populations

The development of a campus-wide retention program requires supportive leadership, the willingness to evoke change on campus, and a careful planning effort. If any of these factors are missing, the chances for success are limited. Ultimate success of a student retention effort depends on the unequivocal support from the office of the president or provost, the involvement of the entire campus in shaping program operations, and the important practice of keeping ideology focused on the student.

Contents

Foreword

In the last decade, the rates of enrollment and retention of certain students of color have declined. Although attention to the need to diversify the student body and create a welcoming climate has increased, success has been limited. In a social and political climate where affirmative action is under attack and the means for ensuring diversity are becoming narrower, we need strategies for retaining students who are able to enter higher education. Over the last few decades, professionals have searched for generalized strategies and techniques to retain students, but often studies have not examined the specific needs of students of color. Because students of color often make up a much smaller percentage of students in studies, their experiences and needs are often lost and go undetected. As Swail, Redd, and Perna describe, the United States will become significantly less white over the next fifty years, so these issues are becoming more urgent.

Retaining Minority Students in Higher Education: A Framework for Success by Watson Scott Swail, with Kenneth E. Redd and Laura W. Perna, is being published at a crucial time: campuses realize they need to make changes yet have few if any strategies to move forward. This monograph, which provides a framework that can fundamentally alter retention and success of all students, begins with a description of the context for students of color, retrenchment of affirmative action, and the reduction in the pipeline of students of color. The authors highlight the need to move from a focus on access, the main thrust of federal policy the last three decades, to success. In the following chapters, the monograph shifts the discussion to what happens once students of color come to college campuses. The heart of the book outlines why students leave college, exploring Tinto's attrition model, Bean's synthetic model, and Anderson's force field analysis. The authors focus on a host of issues such as academic preparation, campus climate, and social integration, presenting a complex picture from the breadth of literature produced in the last thirty years. The framework for retention developed by the authors responds to the host of social, cognitive, and institutional factors identified as issues in the research and are tied to specific support units and services on campuses. Moreover, the framework places the student at the center of the model and focuses on the institutional role in shaping students' experiences, an area where professionals have some level of control. As the authors note, "The strength in the model and the framework that follows is in its ability to help institutions work proactively to support student persistence and achievement."

Programs and services are not enough to ensure success; monitoring student progress is critical. Data and evidence (both quantitative and qualitative) on the success of students must be collected and reviewed on a systemic and ongoing basis. The monograph also underscores the importance of thinking across the entire institution to successfully implement and lead a retention effort. Tinto's seven action principles serve as a helpful strategy. A wealth of promising programs and practices is listed in the appendix. I invite readers to share this monograph with others who care about the success of students of color.

Adrianna J. Kezar
Series Editor

Acknowledgments

This volume is the culmination of several years of research and work, and it would not have happened without the assistance of a number of individuals. I wish to thank the following persons for their hard work and support during this period and this project, in particular the late Dennis Holmes, the George Washington University, for general guidance; Bernard Charles, the McKenzie Group, for helping develop the original research project; Nancy Adelman, SRI International, for her leadership; and Manya Walton, consultant, for her assistance on the literature review.

Special thanks to Ken Redd of NASFAA and Laura Perna of the University of Maryland for their continual goodwill and expert support. They made this volume a much better reference for readers.

A special thanks is due Jorge Balan of the Ford Foundation for sponsoring this project and SRI International for project management. All of us in the education community appreciate the continued support of research and practice with respect to educational opportunity.

Postsecondary Opportunity

A 1975 RESEARCH ARTICLE by Vincent Tinto, "Dropout from Higher Education: A Theoretical Synthesis of Recent Research," spurred more than twenty-five years of dialogue on student retention and persistence in higher education. Though it has been attacked by some and revised by Tinto himself, his work has remained the dominant sociological theory of how students navigate through our postsecondary system.

More than a quarter century later, the issues of student retention and persistence are as pertinent as they were when Tinto first published his student integration model. In the 1970s and 1980s, public policy was focused primarily on access, with federal and state legislation aimed at reducing barriers to higher education. By the mid-1990s, the discussion moved from access to issues of choice, affordability, and persistence. Although gaining entry to college is still a dramatic accomplishment for some, persisting to degree is what really matters in the postcollege world. Unfulfilled academic goals often result in unfulfilled career realities: lower pay, less security, fewer opportunities, and dreams deferred—if not abandoned.

The issue of retention is a persistent problem in higher education. For the past 100 years, the institutional graduation rate has stubbornly held at the 50 percent mark: half of all students entering higher education fail to realize their dreams and aspirations based on earning a certificate or degree. As Tinto remarks, "The consequences of this massive and continuing exodus from higher education are not trivial, either for the individuals who leave or for their institutions" (1993, p. 1).

For students of color in particular, the stakes have never been trivial. Access and completion rates for African American, Hispanic, and Native American students have always lagged behind those for white and Asian students. The same is true for low-income students and students with disabilities (Gladieux and Swail, 1998). But great strides have been made since the War on Poverty of the 1960s. Postsecondary enrollment rates for students of color are at levels similar to those for white and Asian students, although equal access to four-year colleges remains an area of concern, especially at our nation's most selective institutions. But even if access rates for minority students were on a level with majority white students, students of color have not been able to realize the degree production rates of other students. In fact, they earn degrees at a ratio between 1:2 and 1:3 compared with white and Asian students.

Given that the United States will become significantly "less white" over the course of the next fifty years, issues of color cannot be ignored. California is already a "majority minority" state, but its flagship public institutions of higher education have embarrassing low participation rates among African American and Hispanic students. Texas, Florida, and several other states host similar problems. If such issues are not urgently addressed, today's retention and diversity problems will seem like child's play in a few, short decades.

In 2004, the Congress is expected to reauthorize the Higher Education Act of 1965. Congress will likely tinker with Pell Grant authorizations, loan limits and rules, and other important issues such as teacher training and distance education. Another goal of reauthorization may be to pressure institutions to improve student retention and completion, in view of Congress's limited ability to force colleges to curb spiraling tuitions. Beyond such measures, concerted action will be required to spur U.S. colleges, on a large scale, to get more serious about retention and persistence and move faster to become more diversity friendly.

This publication is intended as a reference for key stakeholders regarding the realities of, and strategies for, student retention. It is our hope that it will serve as a compass for those charged with the complex task of improving retention at their campus. More specifically, it details the findings of three levels of research. The first is an exhaustive review of the literature on issues that affect the retention of minority and underrepresented students in postsecondary education. Updating a previous study of minority student retention in the mid-1990s (Swail, 1995), this review looks at more recent issues facing underrepresented students in the college pipeline.

Second, our team analyzed a number of databases to look for enrollment, persistence, and completion trends of students of color at U.S. colleges and universities. We also examined pre- and postcollege issues such as preparation and employment.

Finally, investigators conducted a series of focus groups and interviews with campus leaders and practitioners about current practice and their perspectives on how our nation's campuses are dealing with the problem of student retention.

The analysis and discussion in this monograph focus primarily on the road to and through the four-year college and university. Thus, we have not provided data or discussion on the community college sector, still a vitally important sector of the public postsecondary system in the United States. Because the community college is much different from the four-year college, we believe that a separate publication would do justice to the peculiarities and specificities accorded to the community college and the type of students who attend those institutions. As well, we strongly advise readers not to take our observations of earning power or other returns to a bachelor's degree as the cardinal rule of the economy. The community college likewise provides students with a distinct advantage over those whose highest academic credential is a high school diploma. Still, because the BA is the standard-bearer of postsecondary education and because our research has been focused primarily on that constituency, we believe our discussion is better targeted at that one particular level.

To aid readers, this publication is divided into four sections. This first chapter introduces the key policy issues and presents data on the retention of minority students in the United States. We begin with a discussion of the growing importance of a college degree in America, followed by an analysis of the cost of student attrition to students, colleges, and society. The chapter also presents data on the educational pipeline for minority students and concludes with a synopsis of recent affirmative action legislation.

The second chapter focuses on why students leave college and presents theoretical models that describe student persistence, and the next one introduces a comprehensive framework and geometric model that provides a new perspective on student persistence and achievement.

Finally, the fourth chapter reviews key factors in implementing programs for improving retention on college campuses, including the major role of leadership. Two appendices contain useful collections of information. Appendix A provides information on twenty-five programs and strategies of interest to administrators and practitioners, and Appendix B is an annotated bibliography of studies that we deem important resources.

As stated, the major purpose of the report is to engage higher education personnel in the complex area of student retention through a discussion of important concepts, issues, and practices. We hope that better understanding will lead to increases in diversity and opportunity for all attending postsecondary campuses.

The Growing Importance of a College Degree

> Higher education has an enormous responsibility for our society's well-being. . . . Education determines not only earning capacity but also the very quality of human life. Even longevity is correlated with educational achievement. In the broad sense of how well we live our lives—both individually and collectively—higher education is a public-health issue.
>
> [Davies, 2001]

Education has a profound impact on both the individual and society at large, and it is one of the surest ways to increase one's social and economic levels and overcome the barriers of poverty and deprived social conditions (Swail, 2000). According to the U.S. Census Bureau, individuals with a bachelor's degree earn about 77 percent more than that of high school graduates, and those with a professional degree earn 50 percent more than those with a bachelor's degree (Figure 1). On an annual basis, these variances are considerable. Over a lifetime, they are tremendous. The earning differential between each level is approximately $1 million, not counting investment opportunities and capital gains for those with high levels of disposable income, afforded mostly to those with advanced and professional degrees.

Socioeconomic status is closely related to race and ethnicity. African Americans and Latinos earn considerably less, on average, than white families. In fact,

FIGURE 1
Median Annual Household Income, by Educational Attainment of Householder, 25 Years Old and Over, 1999

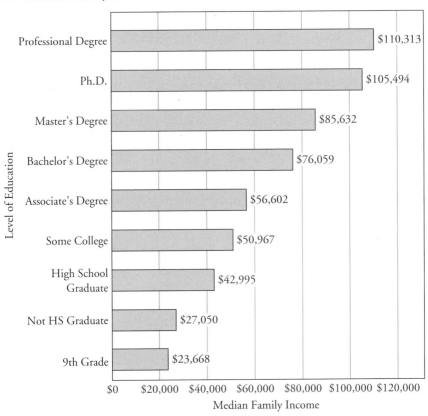

SOURCE: Mortenson (2002).

both groups earn less than two-thirds of what white households earn (U.S. Census Bureau, 2001). Although this lower income directly impacts the ability to make purchases, the greater impact is on an individual's or family's abilities to plan, save, and invest for future security and to invest in their own personal development. In other words, earning power affects the ability to become more capable and competitive and increase one's human and social capital.

Although gaps will always exist in who goes to college and who ultimately succeeds, it still holds true that education has the greatest potential to benefit all. "There are no guarantees in life with or without a college diploma . . . but . . . the odds are increasingly stacked against those with the least education and training. The more education one has, the more—on average—one earns . . . And this relationship has become conventional wisdom. People understand: who goes to college—and often which college— determines more than ever who has entrée to the best jobs and the best life chances" (Gladieux and Swail, 1998, p. 101).

A recent report by RAND suggests that the social/societal benefits of education may exceed the private—or individual—benefits (Vernez, Krop, and Rydell, 1999). This in-depth analysis of national data sets found that increases in education level resulted in improvements in social cohesion, technological innovations, and tangible intergenerational benefits that affect the entire society. In addition, reductions in crime and recidivism, Medicaid and Medicare costs, and other social costs are tied to education levels. The study provides this example of education's benefits:

> *For every native-born Mexican woman who graduates from high school instead of dropping out, the nation would save $2,438 in social programs and would add $1,843 in public revenues in her 30th year. Similar savings and increases in public revenues would accrue annually over her lifetime. In addition, this woman would enjoy $2,588 more in disposable income during her 30th year. If this woman were to attend some college instead of stopping at high school, the result would be $956 more in program savings, $1,398 more in public revenues, and $2,401 more in disposable income at age 30. And graduating from college would add another $411 in program savings, $2,551 in public revenues, and $3,722 in disposable income [Vernez, Krop, and Rydell, 1999, p. 30].*

The fact that Americans in all walks of life understand the importance of education affects educational institutions in two distinct ways. First, the demand for postsecondary studies has increased greatly over the past several decades. Enrollments are up more than tenfold since the mid-1900s to approximately 14 million students each year, with four-year enrollments attracting almost 4 million full-time equivalent students annually. The United States has the largest and broadest postsecondary system in the world, and certainly the most open system (Gladieux, 2001), allowing a full spectrum of individuals from all levels of society to participate. From a purely market standpoint, higher education institutions have done well. Although colleges and universities continue to raise tuition and fees at rates two to three times that of inflation to meet their budgets (College Board, 2002), higher education has done well to meet the market demand.

It is important to note that this increase in demand for education has an economic relationship to academic persistence and completion rates in the United States. For example:

> *There is a linear relationship between enrollment and income. If an institution has a break-even point of one thousand students, maintaining an enrollment of eleven hundred students represents an enormous cushion, since most classes can be 10 percent larger without additional cost to the institution. If the enrollment drops to nine hundred, however, the instructional costs remain the same, but faculty and other institutional employees may be faced with the loss of 10 percent of their income or 10 percent of their colleagues. Given a typical tuition of $5,000 at an institution enrolling eight hundred full-time freshmen where the freshman to sophomore year attrition rate is 25 percent, the loss of two hundred students would cost the school $1 million. Across the country, the tuition loss due to full-time freshman attrition alone would be $3 billion [Bean, 1986, p. 47].*

Bean's example resonates as well today as it did in 1986. The ability of an institution to retain its students relates directly to its budget. The argument has been made that low retention rates (or high attrition rates) drive up the cost of education through inflated tuition and fee charges and increased consumption of public subsidies (at least for public institutions). Tuition, fees, and subsidies are *already* inflated, however, because the cost of attrition has been packaged into those charges that are passed off to the student, family, and taxpayer.

Thus, our inability to reduce attrition during the past fifty years of postsecondary expansion has had—and continues to have—serious implications for the inflationary pressures on tuition and fees at public and private universities across the country. Each fall when the College Board releases its *Trends in College Pricing* report at the National Press Club, members of the media ask why tuition and fees continue to escalate. Typical answers include the costs of technology infrastructure, new housing units, and enhancing the quality of education, but a main driver of these price increases that is rarely discussed is the enormous cost of losing students.

This reality is not lost on managers of educational institutions. During the mid-1990s, one of this report's authors had a discussion with a vice president of student services at one of the more exclusive private universities in the Washington, D.C., area. The vice president calculated that each enrolled student cost the institution about $750 to attract and enroll, including the costs of recruitment, outreach, and admissions. He was concerned about the sizable investment the institution would lose if it let that student fall out of the system—an investment that would not or could not be recouped.

Beyond the sheer financial impact, the implications of retention and attrition are felt in the culture of the institution. Bean (1986) references a connection between high attrition and low faculty morale as well as a sense of failure among students, administrators, and staff. Just as institutions are valued on the basis of their selectivity, students, parents, and policymakers rank institutions in light of their graduation rates. A main indicator in the infamous *U.S. News & World Report* survey is the institutional graduation rate. People want to know whether an institution gets students through. Regardless of an institution's mission and selectivity, schools with low retention and graduation rates carry a burden that has a direct impact on the college's ability to recruit and retain future students. It is a difficult and vicious cycle to break.

Institutions also have an ethical obligation to retain students. By admitting a student, an institution not only makes a contractual commitment to that student but also incurs a moral obligation to provide him or her with an appropriate level of education and support. Through admissions, the institution essentially states, "You belong here, and we're here to help you." Institutions that admit students without providing adequate resources or support are not doing themselves or their students any favors. In fact, in many cases, they could be causing more harm than good. Students who leave before graduation—especially low-income and disadvantaged students—often do so with a sizable loan burden and poor prospects for employment without the degree they originally sought. As a further complication, these students have a high propensity to default on their student loans, affecting their credit rating and digging themselves into a deep financial hole.

Moving from Access to Success

Since World War II, the primary focus of federal support for higher education has been on postsecondary access. The G.I. Bill (the Serviceman's Readjustment Act of 1944) was introduced to help military servicemen reintegrate into the economy and society after the war (as well as to ward off a recession by the influx of hundreds of thousands of workers into the U.S. economy). An astonishing 40 percent of military veterans took advantage of the G.I. Bill, ushering higher education into a new era (Levine and Nidiffer, 1996).

The 1960s brought the War on Poverty and two major legislative packages: The Civil Rights Act of 1964 and the Higher Education Act of 1965. These bills established the tenet for future federal involvement in education, which historically had been a state responsibility. The federal government had already laid the groundwork for access to postsecondary education through the G.I. Bill and through increased focus on math and science education after *Sputnik* in 1957. But the legislation of the mid-1960s expanded the federal role through new student financial aid programs and academic support programs, such as the TRIO programs (Upward Bound, Student Support Services, and Talent Search). As President Johnson said upon signing the Higher Education Act of 1965, "We need to do more . . . to extend the opportunity for higher education more broadly among lower and middle income families." And they did.

The 1970s continued the federal government's expansion into support for educational opportunity, resulting in the Pell Grant (originally known as the Basic Educational Opportunity Grant, or BEOG, before being renamed for Rhode Island Senator Claiborne Pell in 1980). In the words of President

Nixon, this measure was intended to ensure that "no qualified student who wants to go to college should be barred by lack of money" (Gladieux and Wolanin, 1976, p. 70). Later reauthorizations of the Higher Education Act established more programs, with the greatest expansion of aid coming in 1992 through the introduction of the unsubsidized loan programs (Wolanin, 1998).

Federal expansion into education was founded on the generally agreed principle that federal responsibility lay in opening the doors of higher education. A huge expansion of access occurred in the 1990s, driven partially by an economy that needed highly skilled individuals. At the same time, higher education grew considerably more complicated. College was not just about the "traditional" 18- to 24-year-old set anymore; scores of adults began to come back to college or started attending for the first time. In addition, the rise of distance education, proprietary schools, and corporate universities began changing the face of higher education. Education became a market, and even Wall Street took interest.

These changes invariably made the definition of a college student difficult. And it also made the compartmentalization of dropouts, stopouts, repeaters, and transfers more difficult. For instance, of the 67 percent of students who "accessed" postsecondary education in 1982 directly from high school, only 55 percent received some type of degree (BA: 40 percent; AA: 9 percent; certificate: 6 percent). But what happened to the other 45 percent underlines the significance of the persistence issue (Adelman, 1997). Thirteen percent were incidental students with fewer than ten earned credits. Of this group, 60 percent were gone by the end of their freshman year. Twenty-four percent earned fewer than two years' worth of credits, with large percentages of them attending multiple institutions. And 8 percent earned more than 60 credits but received no degree. That's a lot of earned credits with no bankable result.

In 1997, the National Postsecondary Education Cooperative held a conference to "reconceptualize" access in postsecondary education. Vincent Tinto, in his conference white paper, said, "The point of providing students access to higher education is to give them a reasonable opportunity to participate in college and attain a college degree" (Tinto, 1997, p. 1). But that is not always the case, and success and responsibility continue to be defined in terms of access.

As we begin to close in on four centuries of higher education in America, it is perhaps a good opportunity for institutions to reconceptualize their role in society. While our colleges and universities have never been as accessible to the general public as they are now, that openness has, in the words of Levine and Nidiffer, been "passive" (1996, p. 52). Throughout our history, government has intervened at various times to further open access to underrepresented groups. The Morrill Act of 1862 created the land-grant public institution, and thirty years later Morrill Act II provided for historically black colleges and universities (HBCUs) to provide access for the black population, who were not provided access at many land-grant institutions. Given Tinto's comments about access, perhaps now is the time for government to intervene and talk about success rather than open doors. Future public policy needs to focus on prying open the exit doors to our institutions while continuing to open those at the entrance.

Diagnosis by the Numbers: The Education Pipeline for Racial and Ethnic Minorities

Educational opportunity and success are uneven in the United States by income and by race/ethnicity, and African American, Hispanic, and Native American students continue to earn degrees at substantially lower rates than whites and Asians. In 2000, only 11 percent of Hispanics and 17 percent of African Americans in the United States age 25 and older had attained at least a bachelor's degree, compared with 28 percent of whites and 44 percent of Asians (Chronicle of Higher Education Almanac 2001–02, August 31, 2001).

A review of available data suggests that increasing the share of students of color who attain a bachelor's degree requires attention to four critical junctures: academic preparation for college, graduation from high school, enrollment in college, and persistence in college to completion of the bachelor's degree. This section describes the racial and ethnic group differences at each of these four junctures and concludes by describing the importance of raising educational attainment levels for both individuals and society.

Critical Juncture 1: Academic Preparation for College

The first critical juncture on the road to a bachelor's degree is becoming academically prepared during high school to enroll in college and persist to degree completion. Research shows that the level of academic preparation in high school is positively related to high school graduation rates (Cabrera and La Nasa, 2000), college entrance examination scores (Horn and Kojaku, 2001), predisposition toward college (Hossler, Schmit, and Vesper, 1999), college enrollment (Alwin and Otto, 1977; Alexander, Pallas, and Holupka, 1987; Hossler, Braxton, and Coopersmith, 1989; St. John, 1991; Perna, 2000), representation at more selective colleges and universities (Horn and Kojaku, 2001), rates of transfer from a two-year to a four-year institution (Cabrera, La Nasa, and Burkam, 2001), progress toward earning a bachelor's degree by age 30 (Adelman, 2002), college persistence rates (Horn and Kojaku, 2001), and college completion rates (Cabrera and La Nasa, 2000; Cabrera, La Nasa, and Burkam, 2001). Completing a rigorous curricular program during high school appears to be a more important predictor of college persistence than test scores, particularly for African American and Hispanic students (Adelman, 1999).

A smaller share of black and Hispanic high school graduates than of white and Asian high school graduates is academically prepared for college (Berkner and Chavez, 1997). Figure 2 shows that only about one-half of black (47 percent) and Hispanic (53 percent) high school graduates in 1992 were at least minimally qualified to attend a four-year college or university, compared with more than two-thirds of whites (68 percent) and almost three-quarters of Asians (73 percent), according to the college qualification index developed for the U.S. Department of Education (Berkner and Chavez, 1997). The index is based on a student's cumulative grade point average in academic courses, class rank during the senior year of high school, scores on the 1992 National Educational Longitudinal Study (NELS) aptitude tests, and SAT/ACT scores, adjusted for completion of a rigorous program of academic coursework.[1] Analyses of NELS data show that nearly all students (87 percent) who were very highly qualified according to this index enrolled

[1]"Rigorous coursework" was defined as at least four years of English, three years of science, three years of math, three years of social studies, and two years of foreign language.

FIGURE 2

Percentage of 1992 High School Graduates Who Were Qualified to Attend a Four-Year College or University, by Race or Ethnicity

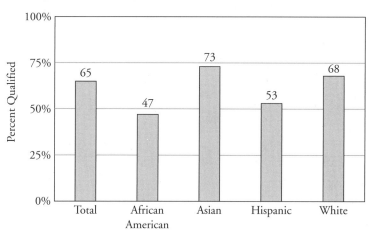

SOURCE: Berkner and Chavez, 1997.

in a four-year college or university within two years of graduating from high school, compared with only 15 percent of those who were marginally or not qualified and 36 percent who were minimally qualified (Berkner and Chavez, 1997).

A rigorous program of academic coursework in high school, including pre-calculus and at least one honors or advanced placement course, also appears to increase the likelihood of college persistence indirectly, as students with a rigorous high school curriculum transfer less frequently to another college or university, attend more selective four-year colleges and universities, and have higher grade point averages during the first year of college (Horn and Kojaku, 2001).

Critical Juncture 2: Graduation from High School

The second critical juncture on the road to a bachelor's degree is graduating from high school. Figure 3 shows that in 2000, 43 percent of Hispanics in the U.S. population age 25 and older had not completed high school, compared with 21 percent of blacks, 14 percent of Asians, and 12 percent of whites.

FIGURE 3

Educational Attainment of U.S. Population Age 25 and Older by Race or Ethnicity, 2000

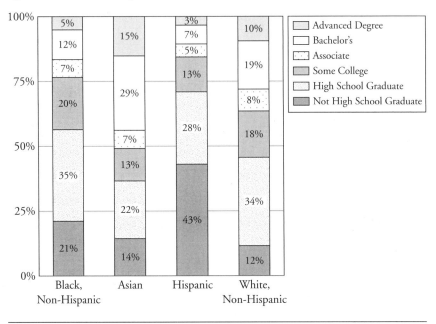

SOURCE: Chronicle of Higher Education Almanac, August 31, 2001.

While useful, examining racial or ethnic group differences in educational attainment among the entire U.S. population age 25 and older may obscure the progress that has been made among younger segments of the population. Figure 4 illustrates the share of the U.S. population between the ages of 25 and 29 that completed at least high school in 1980 and 1999. Among individuals between the ages of 25 and 29, the largest increase in high school graduation rates over the period was among African Americans: from 76.7 percent in 1980 to 88.7 percent in 1999. High school graduation rates also increased among whites, from 89.2 percent to 93 percent. Among Hispanics, high school graduation rates increased only slightly over this twenty-year period, from 58 percent to 61.6 percent. Consequently, although the gap in high school graduation rates between African Americans and whites has narrowed over the past twenty years, the gap between Hispanics and whites has remained virtually unchanged.

FIGURE 4
High School Completion Rates of Persons Age 25 to 29 by Race or Ethnicity, 1980 to 1999

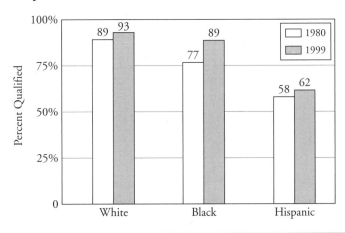

SOURCE: NCES (2001). Digest of Education Statistics 2001, p. 17.

Disaggregating the trends by gender within each racial or ethnic group suggests that high school graduation rates have been comparable for women and men age 25 and older of the same racial or ethnic group over the course of the past two decades. In 1999, comparable shares of white women and white men (about 88 percent), African American women and African American men (about 77 percent), and Hispanic women and Hispanic men (about 56 percent) age 25 and older had completed at least high school.

Together, these data suggest that one source of observed racial and ethnic group differences in educational attainment is lower rates of high school graduation, especially among Hispanic men and women.

Critical Juncture 3: Enrollment in College
A third critical juncture in the road to completion of a bachelor's degree is enrolling in college. Several indicators can be used to illuminate differences related to race and ethnicity.

Percentage of Traditional College-Age Population. One indicator of racial and ethnic group differences in college enrollment is differences in the percentage of the traditional (18- to 24-year-old) college-age population that graduated from high school and enrolled in college. Figure 5 shows that annual college enrollment rates have generally increased among high school graduates between the ages of 18 and 24 for blacks, Hispanics, and whites since the late 1980s (U.S. Department of Education, 2001b). The share of black high school graduates between the ages of 18 and 24 who were enrolled in a degree-granting institution remained virtually unchanged between 1979 and 1989 (28.9 percent versus 29.4 percent) but increased through the 1990s to 39.6 percent in 1999. Similarly, the shares of Hispanic high school graduates between the ages of 18 and 24 who were enrolled in college were comparable in 1979 and 1989 (29.1 percent versus 29.4 percent) but higher in 1999 (32.8 percent). In contrast, the share of white high school graduates enrolled in college increased between both 1979 and 1989, from 31.6 percent to 39.6 percent, and 1989 and 1999, to 46.1 percent (U.S. Department of Education, 2001b).

FIGURE 5

Enrollment Rates of 18- to 24-Year-Old High School Graduates in Degree-Granting Institutions by Race or Ethnicity, 1972 to 1999

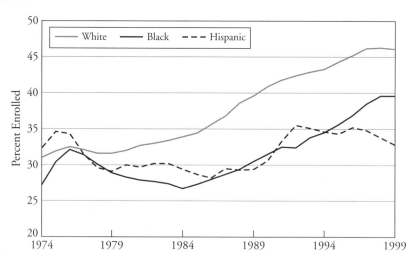

Note: Data adjusted using a three-year rolling average.
SOURCE: NCES (2001). Digest of Education Statistics 2000.

As can be seen in Figure 5, by 1999, large gaps still existed in the enrollment rates of students by race and ethnicity. Black students lagged 6 percent behind white students, and Hispanic students lagged 13 percent behind white students. It is disconcerting that this gap has not been reduced in the past twenty years. More disconcerting is the fact that it appears to be broadening between some groups (U.S. Department of Education, 2001b).

Representation Among Undergraduate Enrollments. A second indicator of racial and ethnic group differences in college enrollment rates is differences in the representation of various racial and ethnic groups among undergraduate enrollments. At four-year colleges and universities, the representation of African Americans and Hispanics attending full time for the first time increased between 1986 and 1997.

Figure 6 shows an increase in representation from 9.4 percent to 11 percent for African Americans and an increase from 3.2 percent to 8.3 percent for Hispanics. Despite this progress, the representation of African Americans and Hispanics among first-time, full-time freshmen at four-year institutions continues to be lower than their representation in the traditional college-age

FIGURE 6
Trends in the Representation of First-Time, Full-Time Freshmen at Four-Year Institutions, 1976, 1986, and 1997

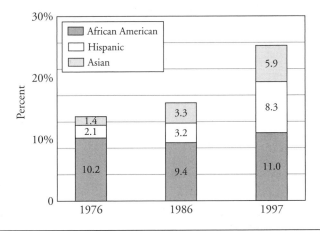

SOURCE: Analyses of Integrated Postsecondary Data Systems, Fall Enrollment Surveys.

population. In 1995, of the traditional college-age population (18 to 24 years old), 14.3 percent was African American and 13.7 percent was Hispanic (Nettles and Perna, 1997).

In addition to being less likely than whites to enroll in a four-year college, African Americans, Hispanics, and Native Americans appear to be more likely to enroll in a two-year institution. Table 1 shows that, unlike whites and Asians, African Americans, Hispanics, and Native Americans represented a higher share of first-time, full-time freshmen attending two-year institutions than of first-time, full-time freshmen attending four-year institutions in fall 1997.

The higher rate of enrollment in public two-year institutions compared with a four-year college or university is problematic for those interested in increasing bachelor's degree completion rates for traditionally underrepresented populations. The reason is the low rates of transfer from public two-year colleges to four-year institutions. Research shows that only 32 percent of whites, 33 percent of African Americans, and 25 percent of Hispanics who first enrolled in a public two-year college in 1995–96 had transferred to a four-year college or university within six years (Berkner, He, Cataldi, and Knepper, 2002).

TABLE 1
Number and Distribution of First-Time Full-Time Freshmen Enrolled in Four-Year and Two-Year Institutions, by Race or Ethnicity, Fall 1997

	Four-year		Public two-year	
	N	%	N	%
Total	1,154,229	100.0%	546,427	100.0%
African American	126,442	11.0%	69,163	12.7%
Native American	9,008	0.8%	8,145	1.5%
Asian	67,893	5.9%	25,817	4.7%
Hispanic	95,600	8.3%	52,342	9.6%
White	831,006	72.0%	381,231	69.8%
Nonresident	24,280	2.1%	9729	1.8%

Source: Analyses of Integrated Postsecondary Education Data Systems, Fall Enrollment Survey, 1997.

Postsecondary Enrollment Within Two Years of Graduation. A third indicator of racial or ethnic group differences in college enrollment rates is provided by data from the National Educational Longitudinal Study of 1988 eighth graders (NELS:88). NELS:88 tracks the educational and occupational experiences of a cohort of students every two years beginning in the eighth grade and into postsecondary education. Analyses of data from the third follow-up study (1994) show that, among individuals who graduated in high school in 1992, a smaller share of Hispanics than of whites and Asians enrolled in some type of postsecondary educational institution within two years of graduating from high school (Berkner and Chavez, 1997). Public two-year college enrollment appeared to be more common among Hispanics than among whites or blacks (Berkner and Chavez, 1997). Figure 7 shows that 34 percent of Hispanics enrolled in a public two-year college within two years of graduating from high school, compared with 25 percent of whites and 23 percent of blacks. More than one-half (54 percent) of Asian high school graduates in 1992 attended a four-year college or university by 1994, compared with only 30.5 percent of Hispanic high school graduates (Berkner and Chavez, 1997).

FIGURE 7
Postsecondary Enrollment by 1994 of 1992 High School Graduates by Race or Ethnicity

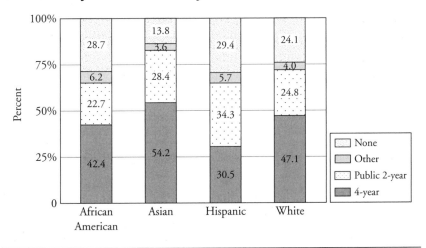

SOURCE: Berkner & Chavez, 1998, p. 7.

Racial and Ethnic Composition of College Attended. A fourth indicator of racial and ethnic group differences in college enrollment is the racial and ethnic composition of the college attended. Understanding the racial and ethnic composition of the undergraduate institution students attend is important, given that racial and ethnic minorities enrolled at predominantly white campuses can face such additional obstacles to persistence as racism, hostility, prejudice, discrimination, a "chilly" climate, institutional bias, negative stereotypes, self-doubt, alienation, isolation, and cultural insensitivity.

As a group, about one-half (53 percent) of African American, Hispanic, and Native American undergraduates attending four-year colleges and universities full-time in fall 1999 were enrolled in a predominantly white four-year college or university, equivalent to about 600,000 students. Analyses of data from the Integrated Postsecondary Education Data System (IPEDS) 1999 Fall Enrollment Survey show that the proportion of full-time undergraduates enrolled in a predominantly white four-year institution ranged from 84 percent of Native American undergraduates to 60 percent of African Americans to 42 percent of Hispanics (see Table 2).

The label for these institutions reflects the racial and ethnic composition of the undergraduate student body. In fall 1999, 92 percent of undergraduates who attended tribally controlled four-year institutions full time were Native American, 89 percent of undergraduates who attended HBCUs full time were African American, and 41 percent of undergraduates who attended four-year Hispanic-serving institutions (HSIs) full time were Hispanic.

Nonetheless, these minority-serving institutions account for only a fraction of the nation's undergraduate enrollments. Fewer than 1 percent of all full-time undergraduates attending four-year colleges and universities nationwide in fall 1999 were enrolled at a tribal institution, 3 percent at an HBCU, and 4 percent at an HSI. Although racial or ethnic minorities are more likely than other undergraduates to attend these institutions, these institutions serve only a relatively small share of racial and ethnic minorities. Only 5.5 percent of Native American full-time undergraduates were enrolled at a tribally controlled institution, 27 percent of African Americans were enrolled in an HBCU, and 21 percent of Hispanics were enrolled at an HSI.

TABLE 2

Undergraduate FTE Enrollment by Race or Ethnicity According to Institution Type and Control, Fall 1999

					FTE Enrollment				
	Total FTE	Non-resident Aliens	Black, Non-Hispanic	Native American	Asian/ Pacific Islander	Hispanic	White, Non-Hispanic	Total Students of Color	Unknown
Public									
HBCU	130,393	1,987	112,812	259	831	959	12,758	114,861	788
Hispanic Serving	203,439	7,343	25,091	2,117	15,333	83,482	61,237	126,023	8,836
Tribally Controlled	2,076	0	1	1,955	0	3	105	1,959	12
Majority Minority	376,433	12,832	33,686	1,660	101,250	99,018	101,807	235,614	26,180
Other	3,432,023	73,724	256,164	32,442	139,306	131,629	2,702,086	559,541	96,672
TOTAL	4,144,364	95,886	427,754	38,433	256,721	315,091	2,877,993	1,037,999	132,487
Private									
HBCU	58,367	1,216	54,364	31	161	304	690	54,861	1,600
Hispanic Serving	40,665	1,967	5,076	198	1,711	15,755	13,266	22,740	2,691
Tribally Controlled	778	0	0	664	0	1	112	665	0
Majority Minority	162,668	9,649	21,913	731	13,948	77,170	32,394	113,762	6,863
Other	1,651,207	59,754	103,328	7,738	75,332	65,913	1,249,621	252,311	89,521
TOTAL	1,913,684	72,586	184,681	9,362	91,153	159,143	1,296,083	444,339	100,675

(Continued)

TABLE 2
Undergraduate FTE Enrollment by Race or Ethnicity According to Institution Type and Control, Fall 1999 (Continued)

					FTE Enrollment				
	Total FTE	Non-resident Aliens	Black, Non-Hispanic	Native American	Asian/ Pacific Islander	Hispanic	White, Non-Hispanic	Total Students of Color	Unknown
All Four-Year Institutions									
HBCU	188,760	3,203	167,176	290	993	1,263	13,447	169,721	2,388
Hispanic Serving	244,104	9,311	30,167	2,314	17,045	99,237	74,503	148,764	11,527
Tribally Controlled	2,853	0	1	2,619	0	5	217	2,625	12
Majority Minority	539,101	22,481	55,599	2,392	115,199	176,187	134,202	349,376	33,043
Other	5,083,230	133,478	359,492	40,180	214,638	197,541	3,951,707	811,852	186,193
TOTAL	6,058,048	168,472	612,436	47,794	347,874	474,234	4,174,076	1,482,338	233,162
Percentage of FTE Enrollment									
Public									
HBCU	3.1	2.1	26.4	0.7	0.3	0.3	0.4	11.1	0.6
Hispanic Serving	4.9	7.7	5.9	5.5	6.0	26.5	2.1	12.1	6.7
Tribally Controlled	0.1	0.0	0.0	5.1	0.0	0.0	0.0	0.2	0.0
Majority Minority	9.1	13.4	7.9	4.3	39.4	31.4	3.5	22.7	19.8
Other	82.8	76.9	59.9	84.4	54.3	41.8	93.9	53.9	73.0
TOTAL	100.0	100.0	100.0	100.0	100.0	100.0	100.0	100.0	100.0

Private

HBCU	3.0	1.7	29.4	0.3	0.2	0.2	0.1	12.3	1.6
Hispanic Serving	2.1	2.7	2.7	2.1	1.9	9.9	1.0	5.1	2.7
Tribally Controlled	0.0	0.0	0.0	7.1	0.0	0.0	0.0	0.1	0.0
Majority Minority	8.5	13.3	11.9	7.8	15.3	48.5	2.5	25.6	6.8
Other	86.3	82.3	55.9	82.7	82.6	41.4	96.4	56.8	88.9
TOTAL	100.0	100.0	100.0	100.0	100.0	100.0	100.0	100.0	100.0

All Four-Year Institutions

HBCU	3.1	1.9	27.3	0.6	0.3	0.3	0.3	11.4	1.0
Hispanic Serving	4.0	5.5	4.9	4.8	4.9	20.9	1.8	10.0	4.9
Tribally Controlled	0.0	0.0	0.0	5.5	0.0	0.0	0.0	0.2	0.0
Majority Minority	8.9	13.3	9.1	5.0	33.1	37.2	3.2	23.6	14.2
Other	83.9	79.2	58.7	84.1	61.7	41.7	94.7	54.8	79.9
TOTAL	100.0	100.0	100.0	100.0	100.0	100.0	100.0	100.0	100.0

Source: Analyses of Integrated Postsecondary Education Data Systems, Fall Enrollment Survey, 1999.

Although about 7 percent of full-time undergraduates nationwide attended a four-year institution that was officially designated a tribal college, HBCU, or HSI in fall 1999, 9 percent of full-time undergraduates attended colleges and universities with a student body that may be characterized as "majority minority." These institutions appear to be relatively more popular with Hispanic and Asian American or Pacific Islander undergraduates; 37 percent of Hispanics and 33 percent of Asians were enrolled in majority minority institutions in fall 1999, compared with 9 percent of African Americans and 5 percent of Native Americans.

Critical Juncture 4: Persistence in College to Bachelor's Degree Completion

The fourth critical juncture on the road to a bachelor's degree is persistence in the selected four-year college or university until the degree program is completed. The lower representation of African Americans, Hispanics, and Native Americans among bachelor's degree recipients than among undergraduate enrollments is one indicator of lower persistence rates for these groups. Figure 8 shows that African Americans received only 9 percent of the bachelor's degrees awarded to U.S. citizens in 1999–00, even though they represented 12.1 percent of U.S. citizen first-time, full-time freshmen enrollments in fall 1999. Similarly, Hispanics accounted for 6.3 percent of bachelor's degree recipients in 1999–00 but 8.1 percent of first-time, full-time freshmen enrollments in fall 1999. Native Americans represented 0.7 percent of bachelor's degree recipients but 1 percent of first-time, full-time freshmen.

Comparisons between the representation among bachelor's degree recipients and undergraduate enrollments are limited because they compare two different groups of students at one point in time. A better indicator of racial and ethnic group differences in undergraduate persistence rates is provided by studies that track the experiences of one group of students over a period of time. The Beginning Postsecondary Student Survey is a nationally representative survey sponsored by the U.S. Department of Education's National Center for Education Statistics (NCES). Figure 9 shows that only 46 percent of African Americans and 47 percent of Hispanics who first enrolled in a four-year institution in 1995–96 with the goal of completing a bachelor's degree actually

FIGURE 8
Distribution of Enrollments and Degree Recipients by Race or Ethnicity, 1999–2000

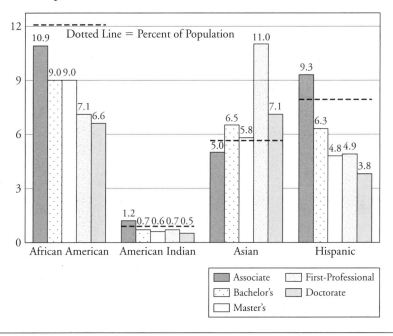

Note: Percentages represent share of U.S. citizens (excludes nonresident aliens from the totals).
SOURCE: Digest of Education Statistics 2001. National Center for Education Statistics 2002.

completed a bachelor's degree within six years, compared with 67 percent of whites and 72 percent of Asians (Berkner, He, Cataldi, and Knepper, 2002).

The rate of completing a bachelor's degree at the institution in which a student first enrolled within six years is higher for students who first enrolled in a private than a public four-year institution, regardless of race and ethnicity. But six-year bachelor's degree completion rates are lower for African Americans and Hispanics than for whites and Asians at both types of institutions. Table 3 shows that only one-third of African Americans (33.6 percent) and Hispanics (34.1 percent) who first enrolled at a public four-year institution completed a bachelor's degree at that institution within six years, compared with nearly half (48.1 percent) of whites and more than half (57.5 percent) of Asians (Berkner, He, Cataldi, and Knepper, 2002).

FIGURE 9
Bachelor's Degree Attainment Rates for Students Who First Enrolled in a Four-Year Institution in 1995–96 with the Goal of Completing a Bachelor's Degree, by Race or Ethnicity

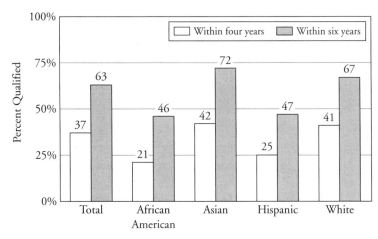

SOURCE: Berkner and Chavez, 1997.

TABLE 3
Percentage of Students Who First Entered a Public or Private Not-for-Profit Four-Year Institution in 1995–96 Who Completed a Bachelor's Degree at That Institution Within Six Years, by Race or Ethnicity

Race or Ethnicity	Total*	Public Four-Year	Private, Not-For-Profit Four-year
Total	55.3%	45.5%	61.0%
African American	40.9	33.6	46.6
Asian	63.8	57.5	69.7
Hispanic	41.3	34.1	48.7
White	59.0	48.1	64.0

Note: Total includes only students who reported that earning a bachelor's degree was a goal.
Source: Berkner, He, Cataldi, and Knepper, 2002.

Importance of Raising Bachelor's Degree Completion Rates

The continued racial or ethnic group differences in bachelor's degree completion have at least three types of implications: (1) differences in economic and noneconomic benefits for different racial and ethnic groups;

(2) less than optimal economic and noneconomic benefits to society; and (3) reduced racial and ethnic group access to advanced degrees and careers.

Differences in Economic Benefits. Continued racial and ethnic group differences in bachelor's degree attainment suggest that a substantially smaller share of Hispanics and blacks than of whites and Asians are able to take advantage of the economic and social benefits associated with earning a college degree. Research shows that individuals who attend and graduate from college realize a number of short-term and long-term economic and noneconomic benefits (Adelman, 1999; Pascarella and Terenzini, 1991). The short-term benefits include enjoyment of the learning experience, involvement in extracurricular activities, participation in social and cultural events, and enhancement of social status. Long-term or future benefits include higher lifetime earnings, a more fulfilling work environment, better health, longer life, more informed purchases, and lower probability of unemployment (Bowen, 1980; Leslie and Brinkman, 1988; McPherson, 1993).

The economic benefits of graduating from college are most clearly evidenced by comparing individual incomes with levels of educational attainment. Figure 10 shows that median earnings increase with the level of education attained, regardless of race or ethnicity. For blacks, median earnings for full-time, year-round workers age 25 to 64 increased from about $24,000 for those whose highest level of education is high school to about $37,000 for those whose highest level of education is a bachelor's degree. For Hispanics, the increase is from $22,600 to about $37,000.

The economic benefits of earning at least a bachelor's degree are also reflected by the substantial decline in poverty rates associated with higher levels of educational attainment. Figure 11 shows that, regardless of race, the share of adults living below the poverty level declines as the level of education attained increases. The benefits to increasing levels of education appear to be particularly dramatic for African Americans. About 34 percent of blacks age 25 and older who have not completed high school are living below the poverty level, compared with only 3 percent of blacks age 25 and older who have completed at least a bachelor's degree.

FIGURE 10
Median Earnings of Full-Time, Year-Round Workers Age 25 to 64 by Educational Attainment and Race, 1999

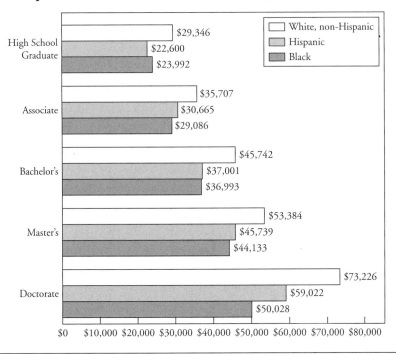

SOURCE: Current Population Survey (2000). PINC-03.

Benefits to Society. Increased levels of educational attainment also produce economic and noneconomic benefits for society at large, including reduced crime, reduced dependency on public welfare and Medicaid, increased volunteerism, higher voting rates, and greater civic involvement (Bowen, 1997). Based on his comprehensive assessment of the public and private benefits of higher education, Bowen (1997) concluded that the single most important effect of higher education is intergenerational, an effect that is manifested most clearly by the increased educational attainment of one's children. A review of the racial and ethnic group differences in educational attainment shows clear differences in the extent to which future generations are benefiting from the educational attainment of their parents.

FIGURE 11
Percent of People Age 25 and Older Below the Poverty Level by Race and Educational Attainment, 1999

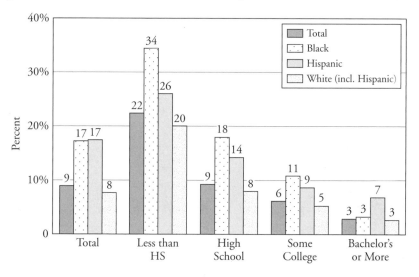

SOURCE: Current Population Survey (2000). Detailed Poverty Package.

Access to Advanced Degrees and Careers. Third, because a bachelor's degree is a prerequisite for enrollment in a professional, master's, or doctoral degree program, continued racial or ethnic group differences in completion of a bachelor's degree mean that the share of African Americans, Hispanics, and Native Americans eligible to enroll in an advanced degree program is necessarily smaller than the share of whites and Asians. The representation of African Americans, Hispanics, and Native Americans declines as the degree level increases. For example, African Americans received 9.6 percent of associate's degrees and 7.8 percent of bachelor's degrees awarded in 1996–97 but only 6.4 percent of master's degrees, 6.5 percent of first professional degrees, and 3.9 percent of doctoral degrees. Hispanics received 8.1 percent of associate's degrees and 6.3 percent of bachelor's degrees awarded but only 3.9 percent of master's degrees, 5.3 percent of first professional degrees, and 2.5 percent of doctoral degrees.

Possession of an advanced degree typically provides access to the highest paying, highest status, most influential careers and occupations (Figure 12). Individuals who complete no more than high school dominate service occupations;

FIGURE 12

Distribution of Employed Persons Age 25 to 64 by Occupation and Educational Attainment, 1999

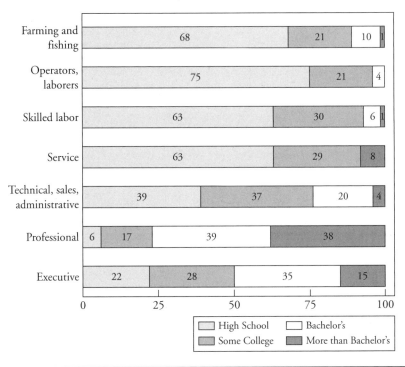

SOURCE: NCES (2001), p. 432.

precision production, craft, and repair; operators, fabricators, and laborers; and farming, forestry, and fishing. In contrast, access to professional specialty occupations is clearly restricted to individuals who possess at least a bachelor's degree. Because smaller shares of African Americans, Hispanics, and Native Americans have attained at least a bachelor's degree, they have less access to these higher status occupations.

Diversity 101: Affirmative Action in America

Most of the attention on the college enrollment experiences of racial and ethnic minority students has focused primarily on those who seek to attend predominantly or traditionally white institutions through diversity or affirmative action programs (Redd, 2001; Reisberg, 2000). Several recent federal court rulings and voter initiatives have eliminated the use of affirmative action programs at a number of public colleges and universities, however, and the substitutes to racial preference programs thus far offered by policymakers may not provide minority students with similar opportunities to attend selective higher education institutions. And although enrollment of minority students has received much of the general public's attention, retention rates of students of color at predominantly white institutions may be a much bigger concern. Thus, the role that minority-serving institutions, particularly HBCUs and HSIs, play in providing educational opportunities may become increasingly more important in the years ahead. But will these institutions have the resources needed to educate an increasing number of minority students?

Affirmative Action, Minority Student Access to College, and College Retention: What Does the Future Hold?

The recent decision by the U.S. Supreme Court allowing the University of Michigan to continue considering race as a factor in student admissions has once again brought affirmative action to the forefront of American higher education. However, while the court's five-to-four ruling in *Grutter v. Bollinger* allows selective colleges and universities to continue to use affirmative action plans to recruit and retain a "critical mass" of African American, Hispanic, and Native American students, it also urges college officials to prepare to dismantle racial diversity plans within twenty-five years (Lane, 2003). On the same day, the Supreme Court's ruling in *Gratz v. Bollinger* struck down the University of Michigan's undergraduate affirmative action admissions plan, which used a point system to rank prospective student applications. The two rulings mean that selective institutions are allowed to use affirmative action programs as long as institutions' admissions officers consider each prospective student's individual characteristics and academic records without using a point or ranking system. That is, race may be a "plus factor" in admissions decisions (Lane, 2003, p. A1).

While proponents of affirmative action hailed the court's decisions as a victory for higher education, opponents believe they will lower standards for graduation, increase dropout and flunk rates, and stigmatize qualified minority students with the presumption that their matriculation is attributable to their race rather than their academic abilities (Levey, 2003). While the Supreme Court's decision has clarified the legality of affirmative action plans for colleges and universities, it has not ended the contentious debate on this issue.

The Supreme Court's recent ruling is just one in a series of legal challenges to the use of racial preferences to diversify college campuses. Prior to the *Grutter* decision, federal court rulings and voter initiatives eliminated the use of affirmative action programs at a number of public colleges and universities, and it was not clear if the substitutes to racial preference programs offered by policy makers would have provided minority students with similar opportunities to attend selective higher education institutions.

Most attention on the college enrollment experiences of racial and ethnic minority students has focused on those who seek to attend predominantly or traditionally white institutions through diversity or affirmative action programs (Redd, 2001; Reisberg, 2000). However, while enrollment of minority students has received much of the general public's attention, retention rates of students of color at predominantly white institutions may be a much bigger concern. Thus, even with the Supreme Court's endorsement of racial preference programs at predominantly white colleges and universities, the role that minority-serving institutions, particularly historically black colleges and universities (HBCUs) and Hispanic-serving institutions (HSIs), play in providing educational opportunities may become increasingly more important in the years ahead. But will these institutions have the resources needed to educate an increasing number of minority students?

This chapter provides a brief history of the use of affirmative action programs in higher education and the legal challenges to diversity initiatives that emerged during the 1980s and 1990s and culminated in the *Grutter v. Bollinger* decision. The study also looks at the alternative policies that states have attempted to use to diversify their college campuses. However, these strategies have not dealt with low minority student retention. Given the controversy surrounding affirmative action, the study also examines the role minority-serving institutions may play in providing educational opportunities to minority students in the years ahead.

A Brief History of Affirmative Action in Higher Education. The term "affirmative action" originates with the administration of President John F. Kennedy. In 1961, he issued Executive Order 10925, which created the Committee on Equal Employment Opportunity (later renamed the Equal Employment Opportunity Commission) and mandated that all projects financed with federal funds take "affirmative action" to "ensure that hiring and employment practices are free of racial bias" (Brunner, 2002). Later, beginning in the administration of President Lyndon B. Johnson, the concept of affirmative action was expanded to include "active measures . . . taken to ensure that blacks and other minorities enjoyed the same opportunities for promotions, salary increases, career advancement, *school admissions, scholarships, and financial aid* that had been the nearly exclusive province of whites. From the outset, affirmative action was envisioned as a temporary remedy that would end once there was a 'level playing field' for all Americans" (Brunner, 2002, emphasis added).

There has never been a complete consensus on exactly what strategies colleges and universities were to use to achieve this "level playing field" in higher educational opportunity. However, eventually affirmative action and racial/ethnic diversity programs in college admissions and financial aid programs were generally accepted by most selective higher education institutions under criteria established by Justice Lewis F. Powell's opinion in the U.S. Supreme Court's 1978 decision *Regents of the University of California v. Bakke*. In *Bakke*, Powell wrote that "[w]hile the goal of achieving a diverse student body is sufficiently compelling to justify consideration of race in admissions decisions under some circumstances" (438 U.S. 265), schools could not use inflexible quotas or numerical goals to reach their diversity targets (Brunner, 2002). For practically the next twenty years, public and private colleges and universities generally considered Powell's opinion in *Bakke* the "law of the land" (Bakst, 2000) and used the Powell standards to implement affirmative action plans in admissions and financial aid to help achieve diversity on campus (Bakst, 2000). However, during the 1990s, a series of decisions by federal appeals courts and voter initiatives challenged the legality of affirmative action programs established under *Bakke*.

Challenges to the *Bakke* Standard.   One of the most important recent legal actions that began to limit the scope of affirmative action plans under *Bakke* was the *Hopwood v. Texas* decision of 1996 (78 F.3d 932), in which the U.S. Fifth Circuit Court of Appeals ruled that the goal of racial diversity was not a "compelling interest" for higher education institutions to use affirmative action in admissions (Bakst, 2000; Pine, 2001). Many observers initially believed that, for all intents and purposes, this decision made it illegal for public higher education institutions in Texas and the other states covered by the Fifth Circuit (Louisiana and Mississippi) to use "race as a factor in admissions, financial aid, or retention programs" (Lum, 1997).

In the fall of 1996, soon after the *Hopwood* decision, California voters approved Proposition 209, which outlawed the use of race in determining admissions to any of the state's public colleges and universities, and in state governmental hiring or contracting (Lynch, 2001). Two years later, voters in Washington state passed Initiative 200 (I-200), which, like Proposition 209, ended the use of racial preferences in state college admissions, hiring, and contracts (Bakst, 2000; Pine, 2001).

In addition, the Florida Board of Regents unanimously approved the "One Florida" plan, which, beginning in the fall of 2001, abolished the use of affirmative action in state college and university admissions and replaced the racial preference programs with a plan that would guarantee admission to the state's four-year public colleges and universities to any Florida high school senior who graduated in the top 20 percent of his or her class (Redd, 2001). And in Georgia, the U.S. Eleventh Circuit Court of Appeals, in *Johnson v. Board of Regents of the University of Georgia,* outlawed an affirmative action plan the university used to recruit minority students. Observers of the *Johnson* decision believed that "even a narrowly tailored race-based admissions process violates the Constitution" (Bean, 2001). And in 1997, Barbara Grutter filed suit against the University of Michigan Law School, claiming that its affirmative action policy allowed minority students with lower grades and test scores to be admitted while she was denied admission. A similar suit against Michigan's undergraduate program was filed that same year by Jennifer Gratz and Patrick Hamacher (Lane, 2003; Williams, 2003).

Two key reasons help explain the push by the federal courts and voters to eliminate affirmative action in higher education. First, some whites believe the policies unfairly keep them out of the most selective undergraduate and graduate school programs. As Cheryl Hopwood, lead plaintiff in the *Hopwood* case, argued, "the [University of Texas Law School] discriminated against me. It gave my spot to a minority student because I happen to be white" (Hentoff, 1997). Such claims of "reverse discrimination" by whites apparently have had some saliency with voters and federal judges in several jurisdictions. Richard Cohen, a columnist for the *Washington Post,* eloquently expresses the frustrations and resentment many whites feel about affirmative action in college admissions: "There is a growing, smoldering anger at a system of perceived racial favoritism. Away from university administrative offices . . . it is widely believed that the undeserving are being admitted, promoted, hired or whatever. Sometimes that happens to be the case" (Cohen, 2002).

Second, some believe affirmative action programs have outlived their usefulness and do not accurately reflect our nation's current racial climate and the gains made by persons of color, particularly African Americans. They believe our country has now reached the "level playing field" envisioned when affirmative action plans were developed forty years ago. This view is best summarized by Cohen (2002):

> *Of course, we all know the reasons for affirmative action. But a program devised to overcome the harmful effects of slavery and Jim Crow cannot persist as if racial discrimination has not abated. The secretary of state [Colin Powell] is black. The national security advisor [Condoleezza Rice] is black. Leaders at AOL-Time Warner [Richard Parsons], American Express [Kenneth Chenault] and Merrill Lynch [E. Stanley O'Neal] are black. So is the president of Brown University [Ruth Simmons]. America has changed. Affirmative action seems more like a patronage system than a way of achieving justice.*

It is almost fifty years since the Supreme Court struck down school segregation in the landmark *Brown v. Board of Education of Topeka* decision of 1954, yet we persist in seeing blacks as victims. The immediate victims of racism are quickly passing, but succeeding generations are considered just as victimized, regardless of circumstances of their birth. Paradoxically, though, the efforts to rectify that discrimination not only uses its methods—preferences based on race—but certifies its reasoning: On account of race, this person cannot compete on his or her own.

The "X Percent" Solution. Despite the gains made by African Americans and other groups over the past four decades, evidence shows very clearly that, in general, racial/ethnic minorities still are less likely to attend a postsecondary education institution, particularly an institution with selective admissions criteria. From 1997 to 2000, the average college participation rates for financially dependent eighteen-to-twenty-four-year-old African American and Hispanic high school graduates were 46 percent and 40 percent, respectively, compared with 64 percent for white non-Hispanics (Mortenson, 2001b). Further, according to preliminary data from the National Center for Education Statistics, just 36 percent of the African American undergraduates and 31 percent of Latinos at four-year colleges and universities in 1999–2000 attended schools classified under the Carnegie Classification system as research or doctoral (generally, these are the institutions with the most selective admissions criteria). Conversely, about 44 percent of white non-Hispanic undergraduates attended research or doctoral institutions (U.S. Department of Education, 2001a).

The gaps between enrollment rates for minority and white students continue to persuade state higher education leaders to seek ways to diversify their college campuses, particularly those with selective admissions criteria, without using affirmative action plans that might be challenged in court. In addition to Florida, education leaders in California and Texas have initiated so-called "x percent solutions," whereby some percentage of each of the respective state's high school graduating class is automatically eligible for admission to a public state university. For example, in California, the top 4 percent of the high school class is now automatically eligible for admission to a campus within the University of California system; in Texas, it is 10 percent (Selingo, 2000). Policy makers hope these plans will attract more students from high schools with large minority populations. California recently went one step further by establishing a "comprehensive review" system that seeks to look beyond traditional measures of high school academic performance, such as grade point averages and scores on the Scholastic Aptitude Test, when determining which students to admit (Pine, 2001).

But the success of these alternatives to affirmative action may be limited. X percent solutions have been criticized for exploiting students at racially segregated high schools without improving the students' educational programs. The plans may also hurt minority students who do well academically at predominantly white high schools, but do not graduate in the required top percentile (Selingo, 2000). Ironically, the x percent solutions may prove to offer a greater benefit to white students. In Florida, for example, white students accounted for 59 percent of the total number of high school seniors in 2000, but made up about two-thirds of the top fifth of the graduating classes. African Americans, on the other hand, accounted for 23 percent of the graduating seniors but constituted just 14 percent of the top fifth (Selingo, 2000). In Texas, enrollments at the University of Texas at Austin and Texas A&M University declined from 1997 to 2003 (Flores, 2003). Soon after the *Grutter* decision was announced, officials at the University of Texas System Board of Regents announced that they were abandoning the state x percent plan in favor of an affirmative action plan that complied with the Supreme Court's *Grutter* standards.

An Expanded Role for Minority-Serving Institutions? Despite the recent Supreme Court decision, there are still potential problems ahead for the future of affirmative action. Opponents of the *Grutter* decision have launched a plan to place anti–affirmative action initiatives similar to those in California and Washington on the ballots of Michigan, Colorado, Missouri, and other localities in time for the 2004 presidential election (Milbank, 2003). Further, some believe the court's ruling is temporary at best, as it leaves diversity plans open to court challenges (McClinton, 2003). Further, neither traditional affirmative action plans nor the x percent solutions address the concerns about minority student *retention* at traditionally white schools. While these programs are designed to increase *enrollment* of students of color at majority-white institutions, some observers are now beginning to question the programs' ability to *retain* these students toward degree completion. Research by Pascarella and Terenzini (1991) has suggested that African Americans at predominantly white institutions are more likely than those at HBCUs to experience high levels of social isolation, alienation, personal dissatisfaction, and overt racism. Because of these factors, it is possible that minority students at predominantly white schools may be at greater risk of leaving their institutions before completing their degree programs.

Indeed, while college enrollments have received much of the attention of the popular media and the courts, the gap in retention rates between white and minority students is often a greater concern. The most recent graduation report from the National Collegiate Athletic Association (NCAA) shows that the six-year graduation rate for African American undergraduates (athletes and nonathletes) at the 321 schools that are members of Division I of the NCAA was just 38 percent. That is, *only 38 percent of the blacks who entered Division I colleges in academic year 1993–1994 as full-time, full-year, degree-seeking freshmen had received a bachelor's degree from their original institutions by August 2000.* The rest had either transferred to a new school, dropped below full-time attendance status, took longer than six years to graduate, or dropped out of higher education altogether. The graduation rate for white students was 59 percent, and for Hispanics the rate was 46 percent (NCAA 2001a). At the 295 institutions that are members of NCAA Division II, which tends to have less selective undergraduate admissions criteria, the graduation rate for degree-seeking African American undergraduates was just 32 percent, versus 45 percent for white students and 39 percent for Hispanic (NCAA, 2001b).

The situation for policy makers who seek to increase minority enrollments at traditionally white schools therefore still appears to be precarious, despite the *Grutter* decision. They still face potential legal and voter challenges to the use of affirmative action programs and policies, perceived inadequacy of the alternative diversity strategies, perceptions of white institutions as being inhospitable to students from different racial/ethic groups, and low graduation rates among Latino and African American undergraduates. In the face of these challenges, minority-serving institutions—particularly HBCUs and HSIs—could play an even more important role in providing higher educational opportunities to minority students.

Minority-serving institutions have a history of successfully educating a number of African American and Latino students who otherwise could not have received a college degree (Merisotis and O'Brien, 1998). HBCUs account for just 4 percent of all the four-year colleges and universities in the United States, but they enroll 26 percent of all African American students and produce 28 percent of the black bachelor's degree recipients (Redd, 2001). Similarly, HSIs account for 52 percent of the total Latino postsecondary education student enrollment and 41 percent of the baccalaureate recipients (U.S. Department of Education, 2001b).

While minority-serving institutions have a demonstrated record of success (Merisotis and O'Brien, 1998), they still face two daunting challenges. First, when compared with many predominantly white institutions, many HBCUs and HSIs have fewer financial and other resources. In 1996, the most recent year of available data, the average endowment at historically black colleges was $4 million (equivalent to $2,960 per full-time equivalent student). The average endowment at all other four-year colleges and universities was $67.4 million, equivalent to $15,329 per full-time equivalent student (Sallie Mae, 1999). Additionally, many of the students at HBCUs and other minority-serving institutions come from low-income backgrounds and are the first in their families to enter postsecondary education. These students often need additional financial aid, tutoring, and mentoring programs in order to succeed. A number of HBCUs and HSIs simply do not have these additional resources, and as a result some have higher-than-average attrition rates (Sallie Mae, 1999).

Where Do We Go from Here?
The limits to affirmative action and x percent plans could not have come at a more challenging time for all higher education institutions generally and minority-serving institutions particularly. Demographic projections show that the number of Latino high school graduates will jump 67 percent over the

next ten years, and the number of African American graduates will grow 17 percent (WICHE, 1998). Many of these students will want to attend post-secondary education after their high school years. Will the HBCUs and HSIs be able to expand their course offerings and facilities to meet the increased need? Given the relatively small number of HBCUs and HSIs, it does not appear very likely that they, by themselves, can meet this coming tide of new students. At the same time, data from the National Center for Education Statistics (U.S. Department of Education, 2001a) show that African American and Latino high school graduates enroll in postsecondary education at lower rates than whites. What role can minority-serving institutions play in reversing this trend?

Two recent shifts in student financial aid may also adversely affect future postsecondary education enrollments among minority groups. First, over the past twenty years, more financial aid has been provided in the form of loans instead of grants. According to the College Board (2001), in 1980–1981, 55 percent of all student financial assistance was provided in the form of grants, and 43 percent was in loans (the remainder was work-study). By 2000–2001, the share of aid from grants had fallen to just 41 percent, with the percentage from loans rising to 58 percent. This trend may harm college access for prospective students from low-income families generally and people of color specifically because they tend to be more averse to borrowing student loans than white students and those from higher income families (St. John, 2001).

Additionally, more and more of the available grant aid has been delivered in the form of merit scholarships, which base awards on students' high school grade point averages and other criteria instead of demonstrated financial need. Since 1990, the total amount of state merit-based scholarships grew 206 percent, but the amount of state need-based grants increased only 41 percent (National Association of State Student Grant and Aid Programs, 2001), and total spending for institutional merit scholarships and other "non-need" grants nearly doubled from 1989 to 1995 (Heller, 2001b). African American and Hispanic students are much less likely to meet the criteria necessary to benefit from the additional state merit-aid programs (Heller and Rasmussen, 2001).

These challenges may limit the ability of the HBCUs, HSIs, and other minority-serving institutions to support the larger number of students hoping to enter higher education. While most institutions, especially private colleges and universities, still can now use the Grutter decision standards to design and implement affirmative action programs to diversify their campuses, it may be only a matter of time before new challenges to diversity programs will force institutions to come up with a new standard to close the gaps in college enrollment and retention.

Why Students Leave College

THE LITERATURE REGARDING MINORITY STUDENTS' dropping out abounds with details of why and when students leave college. Many of the studies and literature reviews summarize similar sources and thus supply similar conclusions. Landmark studies by Tinto (1975), Pantages and Creedon (1978), Cope and Hannah (1975), Lenning, Beal, and Sauer (1980), and, more recently, Tierney (1992), Cabrera, Nora, and Castaneda (1993), and Cabrera and La Nasa (2000), have shaped how researchers and practitioners view the issue of student retention and departure. In particular, Tinto's attrition model has become a foundation for most research regarding student departure.

Models of Student Progression

There are several models that depict how students flow through postsecondary education. To provide a foundation for our discussion, we will showcase three leading models here.

Tinto's Student Integration Model

Tinto's theoretical model (1975) was derived from previous work by Spady (1970). Spady, like Tinto a sociologist, presented one of the early conceptual models of the student attrition process in higher education. Based on Durkheim's theory of suicide, Spady suggested that suicide is more probable when individuals are poorly integrated into the shared structure and theorized that the social integration of students (shared group values, academic performance, normative congruence, and support of friends) increases that student's institutional commitment, ultimately reducing the likelihood of student attrition. Tinto (1975) expanded Spady's theory to the process of student integration into the academic and social systems of a higher education institution. His aim was to clarify the effect of multifaceted interactions within the system on student persistence. "It is the interplay between the individual's commitment to the goal of college completion and his commitment to the institution that determines whether or not the individual decides to drop out" (Tinto, 1975, p. 96).

Briefly, Tinto's student integration model consists of six characteristics (see Figure 13). Before matriculation to postsecondary education, students develop certain attributes that are shaped by their familial upbringing. They also develop academic and social skills and abilities in both formal and informal settings. These skills and abilities in turn help form students' goals and commitments regarding college, the workforce, and their place in society as a whole. During college, formal and informal college experiences influence the student's level of integration into the college, academically and socially. According to Tinto, this level of integration has an impact on the student's development of goals and commitments, resulting in either a decision to persist in or depart from college. Essentially, the match between student characteristics and institution shapes students' goal commitments, which in turn influence persistence (Allen, 1994).

Tinto's model refocused the higher education community's understanding that persistence is the outcome of the interaction between students and their experiences in the campus environment (Brower, 1992). Although Tinto's model accounted for student characteristics and campus experiences, it failed to include the interactions of students' off-campus academic and social systems (Tinto, 1982). Tinto acknowledged that these external, not-related-to-college variables might force students to reassess educational goals and commitment to the institution. He failed, however, to address in detail the impact of external campus factors such as finances, family obligations, and external peer groups in his student dropout model (Cabrera, Castaneda, Nora, and Hengstler, 1992; Tinto, 1982). Tinto also recognized that finances might have both long- and short-term and direct and indirect effects on college persistence.

FIGURE 13
Tinto's Longitudinal Model of Institutional Departure (Student Integration Model)

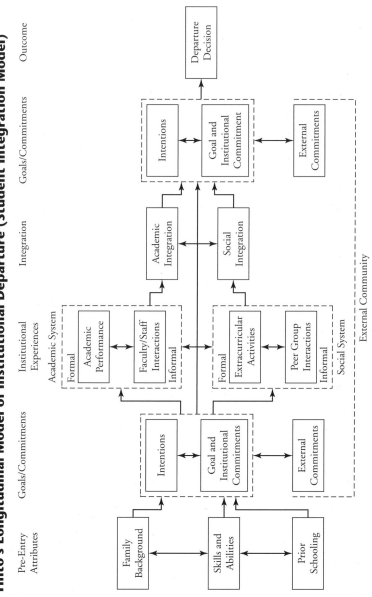

SOURCE: Tinto, 1993, p. 114.

In 1988, Tinto expanded his view of student dropouts to include a three-stage process: separation, transition, and incorporation. This model was adapted from Van Gennep's social anthropology theory, drawing a parallel between the movement of an individual from one group to another in tribal societies with the departure of a student from home and his or her incorporation into the new college community (Fernandez, Whitlock, Maring, and VanEarden, 1998; Tinto, 1988). The *separation stage* refers to the student's parting from past habits and patterns of associations. Tinto suggests that for students to consider themselves part of the college community, they must in a sense leave their former communities. During the *transition stage,* students cope with stresses of departing from the familiar while not completely understanding or integrating into the new college environment. The *incorporation stage* reflects students' competency as an institutional member. After incorporation, the student is no longer the person he or she once was; he has in effect become a new individual. This expanded view adds a time dimension in the form of longitudinal stages of the integration process (Figure 13) that specifically addresses the early stages of separation and transition and the sorts of difficulties students typically face academically and socially before their incorporation into campus life. Lack of integration into the college campus may also result from students' inability to separate themselves from past associations to make the transition to the new community (Tinto, 1988).

Bean and Eaton's Psychological Model

Tinto's model has been revised or enhanced by a number of researchers (Bean, 1982; Stage, 1989; Brower, 1992; and Peterson, 1993). Bean (1982, 1986; Eaton and Bean, 1995; Bean and Eaton, 2000) used important aspects of Tinto's academic and social integration theory in the development of a psychological rather than sociological model (see Figure 14). The purpose, according to Bean, was to help others "visualize how individual psychological processes can be understood in the retention process" (Bean and Eaton, 2000, p. 55).

Bean's model is based on the organizational process models of turnover, which emphasize the significance of behavioral intentions. Intentions to persist are influenced by students' attitudes, which are shaped by their experiences

FIGURE 14
Bean and Eaton's Psychological Model of College Student Retention

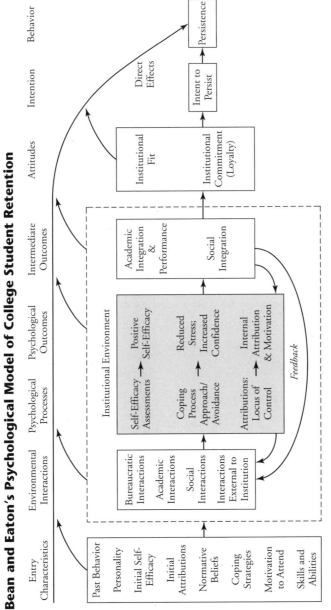

SOURCE: Bean and Eaton, 2000, p. 57.

with the institution. Bean's model incorporates background, organizational, environmental, attitudinal, and outcome variables.

Bean introduced students' intention to stay or leave into the attrition model, derived from psychological theories of Ajzen and Fishbein (1972, 1977) and further developed by Bentler and Speckart (1979, 1981). The theorists argue that a strong correlation exists between attitudes, intentions, and behavior in students and that behaviors and attitudes often reflect one's intentions (Bean, 1986; Eaton and Bean, 1995). Thus, a student's attitude regarding college tends to influence the intent to persist or drop out.

Eaton and Bean (1995) injected coping behavior into previous attrition models to help explain a student's adaptation to the campus structure. The ability to adapt to the campus environment is a reflection of the student's ability to cope, which is directly related to the repertoire of coping skills learned from his or her experiences. "Coping is also dependent upon the situation, timing, and the behaviors with which the individual is familiar and comfortable" (p. 619). Both Bean and Tinto note the level of academic and social integration into the campus structure as indicators of an individual's adaptation to college life. "Adaptation, as measured by social and academic integration, should be an attitudinal reflection of a student's intention to stay or leave the institution . . . ultimately linked to the student's actual persistence or departure" (p. 620).

Shortcomings of the Models

In 1992, Cabrera, Castaneda, Nora, and Hengstler looked at both Tinto's student integration model and Bean's model of student departure and found that a blend of the two models provided a more comprehensive understanding of persistence than either theory alone. As well, they incorporated finances into the student retention model. Although they found no significant direct effect of finances on student attrition, they found an indirect effect through intervening variables like students' academic integration, socialization, and resolve to persist in college.

As Cabrera, Castaneda, Nora, and Hengstler's study suggested (1992), Tinto's and Bean's models are not mutually exclusive and have more similarities than differences. Both models argue that precollege characteristics are determinants of college behaviors and actions, that the student/institution fit are important issues, and that persistence is a result of a complex set of interactions (Hossler, 1984). But the research community, while embracing these theoretical models, has limited its enthusiasm because of the lack of empirical evidence to substantiate their effectiveness in describing the process of student integration and departure from college. A recent review of empirical analysis of Tinto's theory (Braxton and Lien, 2000) sorted published studies into two categories: supportive or unsupportive. Although there was evident support for the theory in several areas, the authors concluded that there was not enough empirical support to substantiate much of Tinto's theory.

A number of authors suggest that Tinto's theory, and specifically his use of Van Gennep's social anthropology theory, is severely limited when applied to minority students (Tierney, 1992; Rendón, Jalomo, and Nora, 2000). To think that students, especially students of color, must or will disassociate from their culture, belief system, and familial support network to become integrated and accepted into their new life on a college campus is difficult to swallow; the reality is more complex. "Nontraditional students often have to negotiate a new landscape, learn how to step in and out of multiple contexts, engage in double readings of social reality and move back and forth between their native world and the new world of college—all at an accelerated pace. Nontraditional students live in multiple realities and lead cyclical lives that demand a high degree of biculturalism" (Rendón, 1996, p. 19).

Rendón, Jalomo, and Nora (2000) suggest that minority and other underrepresented student populations live in a process of biculturation (Valentine, 1971), where individuals live simultaneous lives in two cultures, two realities. Duster calls it "dual competency," where students must be competent in their own culture plus the culture of the institution (Rodarmor, 1991). Troy Duster, a former University of California sociologist, saw it not only as a minority issue but also one that affects white students. "For the first time, our White students are having to navigate their way through cultural mine fields. They're encountering new terrain, and they don't know what it's all about. They're getting their hands slapped, metaphorically. They're getting a dose of wake-up reality. But in a remarkably important way . . . they're getting an education.

And it may be a more important one than they're getting in some of our classrooms" (Duster, quoted in Rodarmor, 1991, p. 44).

Anderson's force field analysis of college persistence (1985) illustrates the many and various factors that researchers, including those just mentioned, identified (see Figure 15). Anderson's model integrates factors that are both external and internal to the student. Although other studies (Lenning, 1982; Bean, 1986) are more comprehensive in identifying factors, Anderson's model provides a representation of the factors in an easy-to-grasp model.

As a final observation, it is important to keep in mind that the human condition is far too complex—as is our system of postsecondary education—to definitely prove the validity of one psychological or sociological theoretical model over another. The theories reviewed in this chapter are useful in describing retention and attrition for students, but they always do so with the full knowledge and understanding that one size does not fit all.

FIGURE 15
Anderson's Force Field Analysis of College Persistence

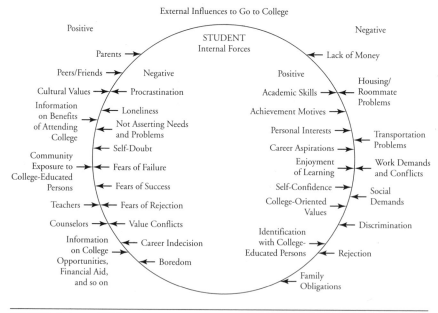

SOURCE: Anderson, 1985.

Factors Related to Retention

As the previous discussion pointed out, there are a number of factors related to retention, and researchers have found differences, as well as similarities, between white students and students of color.

Academic Preparedness

Academic integration and preparation are primary features of many models of retention. Research shows that between 30 and 40 percent of all entering freshman are unprepared for college-level reading and writing (Moore and Carpenter, 1985) and that approximately 44 percent of all college students who complete a two- or four-year degree enrolled in at least one remedial course in math, writing, or reading (U.S. Department of Education, 2001a, p. 49). Without the prerequisite skills needed to survive the rigorous curricula of most college campuses, many students underachieve and leave college during their freshman year or before their sophomore year begins (Astin, 1975; Tinto, 1975; Richardson and Skinner, 1992).

The educational community often defines *academic preparedness* on the basis of students' precollege academic performance as measured by one or more of high school GPA, high school rank, college entrance test scores (specifically math scores), high school college preparatory courses, advanced placement courses, the quality of high school attended, and quality and intensity of high school curriculum. A number of research studies have correlated academic preparedness of minority and nonminority students with their persistence and college completion rates (Adelman, 1999; Borman, Stringfield, and Rachuba, 2000; Fiske, 1988; Parker, 1997; Richardson, Simmons, and de los Santos, 1987), but once the variables related to academic preparedness were controlled, the effects of ethnicity on college persistence disappeared (St. John, Kirshstein, and Noel, 1991). Still, high school GPAs accounted for only 9 percent of the variation in college GPAs for African American students, compared with 25 percent for white students, suggesting that factors other than academic preparedness influence students' college achievement and persistence (Hall, 1999). Other studies also found significant correlations between academic preparation and persistence for low achievers (Porter, 1989) and Hispanic students (Astin, 1982), further supporting Tinto's theory of academic integration and college persistence.

The following survey of major research studies illustrating gaps in academic preparedness by ethnicity focuses on the two key indicators of academic proficiency and college readiness.

The SAT Comparison. The SAT-I is the mainstay of high-stakes tests in America. More than 2 million students sit for the SAT-I each year, while another million-plus take the ACT test. These tests have been highly discussed over the past few years, and the recent passage of President Bush's education plan will subject the nation's children to even more high-stakes testing. A number of researchers and experts have argued the efficacy of these tests (Steele, 1999; Jencks and Phillips, 1998; Guinier, 2001). The University of California, the largest user of the SAT-I, announced that it will stop using the test and will replace it with a subject-based test by 2006. Considering that California is the largest user of SATs in the United States, this move ultimately forced the College Board to announce the development of the "SAT05" in 2002, to be prepared for use in 2005. Nevertheless, the SAT-I is still the prime gatekeeper for our nation's selective and moderately selective four-year colleges.

Consistent findings on the SAT-I show that ethnic minority and low-income students score well below white and Asian students. The most recent data available on the SAT from the 2001 college-bound seniors database verify this long-standing finding. Table 4 provides a comparison, by ethnicity, on the relative scoring on the SAT-I verbal and mathematics tests. As can be seen in the table, ethnic minorities, with the occasional exception of Asian students, score considerably lower on both the verbal and math portions of the test. African American and Mexican American students, respectively, averaged 96 and 78 points lower than white students on the verbal portion of the SAT, and 105 and 73 points lower on the math portion.

The SAT-I instrument has a statistical mean of 500 (standard deviation = 100), which means that approximately half of the total SAT population will score above 500 and half below 500 in any given year or test sitting. A second look at the 2001 scores (not illustrated in Table 4) finds that approximately two-thirds of white students score above 500 on both verbal and math tests, while only a quarter of African American students, a third of Mexican American students, and slightly less than half of Native American students do the same.

TABLE 4
SAT Verbal and Math Scores by Ethnic Group, 2001

Ethnic Group	Verbal Scores			Math Scores		
	Verbal Score	+/− Versus White	Percent above 600*	Math Score	+/− Versus White	Percent above 600*
White	529	—	25%	531	—	27%
African American	433	−96	6	426	−105%	5
Native American/ Alaskan Native	481	−48	15	479	−52	14
Asian/Pacific Islander	501	−28	23	566	+35	43
Hispanic	451	−78	8	458	−73	9

Note: Out of 800 possible points.
Source: College Board, 2001.

As shown in Table 4, raising the standard higher reveals more dramatic findings. Approximately 25 percent of white students register a score above 600 on the SAT (theoretically, about 16 percent of all students would score above that level given a normal curve). With the exception of Asian Americans and Pacific Islanders, who either equal or surpass these marks on the verbal and math tests, only a low percentage of ethnic minority students reach this higher level.

National Assessment of Educational Progress. More commonly referred to as the "nation's report card," the National Assessment of Educational Progress (NAEP) reports every two years in the areas of reading, math, and science.[2] Since 1969, reading, mathematics, science, writing, U.S. history, civics, geography, and the arts have been assessed periodically.

As Table 5 illustrates, very small percentages of black, Hispanic, and Native American students score at proficient levels in reading, math, and science. Only one in twenty-five African American students and one in seventeen

[2]Although NAEP testing occurs on a two-year basis, the reading, math, and science tests are rotated so that each test is conducted on a six-year rotation.

TABLE 5

Percentages of Twelfth-Grade Students Within the Proficient and Advanced Achievement Ranges on the NAEP 1998 Reading Test, 1996 Math Test, and 1996 Science Test

	Proficient			Advanced		
	Reading	*Math*	*Science*	*Reading*	*Math*	*Science*
White	40%	18%	24%	7%	2%	3%
Black	17	4	4	1	0	0
Hispanic	24	6	6	2	0	1
Asian	33	26	19	6	7	3
Native American	24	3	10	3	0	0

Source: College Board, 1999, Table 1, p. 7.

Hispanic students are proficient in math or science, compared with at least one in five white students. Almost no black or Hispanic students register on the advanced level. Considering that reading ability is a primary factor in an individual's ability to learn (Adelman, 1999), the scores in Table 5 are not comforting indicators of the preparedness of these students.

A similar analysis using the NELS data set found that significant gaps in reading and mathematics achievement between white and black students were already in place by eighth grade (U.S. Department of Education, 1997). The difference between white and black twelfth-grade students in reading was reported at 6.1 percentile points, but at the eighth-grade level, the difference was already 5.2 percentile points. This finding suggests that the academic damage was done before any of these students even thought about college. "By the time students get to the 12th grade, it is too late to improve college eligibility or to increase the numbers of students who are ready for college. In fact it could be said that students begin to drop out of college in grade school" (Rendón, 1997, p. 7).

Interestingly, when NCES researchers controlled for reading level, the differences between white and black students fell to 0.8 percentile point, almost negating any gap in learning. Similar differences in reading scores were found for Hispanic students versus white students. The same outcome held true for mathematics.

Course Selection and Integrity. In an attempt to further understand the effect of academic preparation on college persistence, Adelman (1999) developed a composite measure for precollege academic content and performance. Using transcript information in the High School and Beyond database (1982–1993), Adelman verified and accurately mapped high school and college courses. This unique and rich analysis has many implications for policymakers and practitioners, the most significant of which is that a rigorous (or as Adelman asserts, "intensive") mathematics curriculum path taken in high school results in high achievement levels for *all* students, regardless of race or ethnicity.

Several studies point to the academic deficiencies among many minority students, particularly the inability of the school system to better serve underrepresented students (McDermott, Piternick, and Rosenquist, 1980; Fullilove and Treisman, 1990; Berryman, 1983; Astin, 1982; Quality Education for Minorities, 1990). Astin (1982) has attributed much of the poor preparation of minority students to the poor quality of elementary and secondary education, while Berryman (1983) suggests that the public schools do not seem to serve any students particularly well in mathematics and science. Exposure to higher-order skill development is also a concern. As a result of lack of such exposure, students have not "developed the reasoning skills that are necessary for acquiring science concepts, for organizing them into a conceptual framework, and for applying them in appropriate situations" (McDermott, Piternick, and Rosenquist, 1980, p. 136).

A study of NAEP science scores of seventeen-year-olds emphasized this lack of higher-order skills. The study found that although 9 percent of white students had the ability to integrate specialized scientific information, only 0.5 percent of African Americans and 1 percent of Hispanic students demonstrated this ability (Association of American Medical Colleges, 1992). Further exacerbating this issue is the perception that minority students cannot succeed in these higher-order disciplines. Bean (1986) found that teachers who thought this way were more likely to send negative messages to their students regarding their ability in math or science.

Aside from the development of higher-order thinking skills, many minority students lack other critical skills essential to their success in college (Association of American Medical Colleges, 1992; Epps, 1979; Halpern, 1992). Reading, writing, test-taking, vocabulary, and study skills are often barriers to minority persistence in college. The underdevelopment of these skills severely hampers a student's ability to persevere through the onslaught of new information on a daily basis in college.

High school students' course selection is a key variable in both the desire of a student to pursue study in the sciences and the preparedness of the student to persevere in postsecondary study. Studies by Fullilove and Treisman (1990) and Anderson (1989) found that African American students were less likely than their white counterparts to take advanced courses, especially in physics and chemistry. Additionally, Anderson found that African American students scored nearly 70 points below the national norm on achievement tests in physics, biology, and chemistry, and were underrepresented in college preparatory courses, based on their representation in the population. The limited access of these "gatekeeper" courses to minority students severely hampers their chances of achievement in the sciences, or even the likelihood that they will select or persist in such courses.

Many of the minority students who make it over the college admissions hurdle arrive on campus only to find they do not possess the requisite academic skills to succeed. Thus, a high percentage of these students end up on the remedial (developmental) track. As mentioned previously, almost half of all college graduates take at least one remedial class during their college experience. That alone is not a negative finding. In fact, as Figure 16 illustrates, the difference in completion rates between students who took one remedial course (not in math or reading) and those who did not take any remediation was only 1 percent. The problem is deficiencies in reading. "Deficiencies in reading skills are indicators of comprehensive literacy problems, and they significantly lower the odds of a student's completing any degree" (Adelman, 1996). When the remedial college course happens to be reading, completion rates drop to 34 percent.

The data examined here are not an indictment of our nation's children. Rather, they are an indictment of a system that has been unable to rectify inequities in how it educates *all* students, not just those from the higher rungs of the economic ladder or those with an educational legacy that opens up their

FIGURE 16
Remedial Course Experiences of Postsecondary Education Students Who Completed Two- or Four-Year Degrees, 1980–93

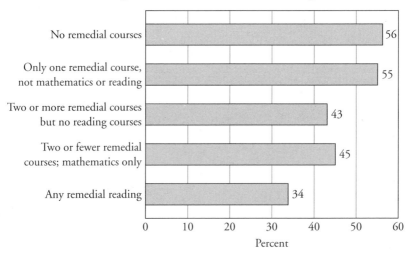

SOURCE: U.S. Department of Education (2001). The Condition of Education, p. 49.

future educational options. Wading through the countless research articles brings one to believe that the most significant factors in whether students are prepared for and motivated to enroll in college is the rigor of their precollege curriculum and the support of peers, family, and friends—regardless of race, ethnicity, gender, income, or almost any other background variable.

Campus Climate

Although researchers tend to agree that institutional fit and campus integration are important to retaining college students to degree completion, campus climate mediates undergraduates' academic and social experiences in college. The normal challenges associated with maneuvering through the college system are stressful to most students; however, minority students at predominantly white institutions (PWIs) encounter additional stresses that come from being a minority. Smedley, Myers, and Harrell (1993) found that minority students at PWIs experienced stress on five separate factors, including social climate, interracial stresses, racism and discrimination, within-group stresses, and achievement stresses. Students identified several major issues:

- Not enough professors of my race
- Few students of my race
- Racist institutional policies and practices
- Difficulty having friendships with nonminorities
- Rude and unfair treatment because of race
- Discrimination
- People close to me thinking I'm acting "white"
- Doubts about my ability to succeed in college

Minority students who are inadequately prepared for such nonacademic challenges can experience culture shock. Lack of diversity in the student population, faculty, staff, and curriculum often restricts the nature and quality of minority students' interactions inside and outside the classroom, threatening their academic performance and social experiences. Qualitative data on African Americans who attend PWIs suggest the availability of ethnic and cultural organizations and a "critical mass" of African American students help reduce the isolation and alienation often found on predominantly white campuses (Hall, 1999). At the same time, Tracey and Sedlacek (1985) argue that noncognitive factors like self-concept, an understanding of racism, and the ability to use coping mechanisms can have a positive effect on students' academic performance and persistence in college.

The research literature shows that HBCUs support campus climates that foster students' self-pride and confidence and lead to academic and social success. Although most African Americans at HBCUs do not experience culture shock associated with race, they do experience the culture shock of transitioning from a secondary educational system to a higher educational one. These institutions traditionally have used holistic approaches for developing students intellectually and socially. Activities have ranged from precollege outreach programs to extensive academic and career counseling (Reyes, 1997). One characteristic of many HBCUs that has remained constant throughout the institutions' history is the personal academic relationships that faculty at HBCUs establish with their students. This characteristic partially explains the tendency of HBCU students—despite any academic and economic difficulties—to demonstrate higher levels of psychosocial adjustment, academic gains, and greater cultural awareness than do their African American counterparts at PWIs (Himelhock, Nichols, Ball, and Black, 1997). As the non–African American student population at HBCUs continues to increase, however, they also must ensure that a nurturing campus climate exists for all students, regardless of race and ethnicity (Swail, 1995).

Unfortunately, the biased practices of many PWIs inadvertently contribute to minority students' cultural shock and alienation. Just (1999) argues that racial climate influences almost every aspect of minority students' college experience, leading to academic and social marginalization. Gonzalez (1999) reported that two Chicano males attending a western PWI felt that the institutional members at large trivialized their culture by not accepting their styles of bilingual communication, dress, and music, and by excluding physical and academic representations of their culture. In addition to marginalizing minority cultures, pervasive racial remarks demean ethnic minorities on campus. Tolerence.org, a Web site operated by the Southern Poverty Law Center to monitor and promote racial and cultural tolerance, estimated 1 million incidents of bias occur every year on our national campuses, with the majority of them unreported to the authorities. Liu and Liu (2000) characterize the alienation of minority students on campus as a structural rather than an individual issue, making colleges and society in general partially responsible for these students' lack of college persistence.

Empirical studies investigating students' perceptions of and satisfaction with campus climate are ambiguous. Ancis, Sedlacek, and Mohr (2000) found that African Americans and Asians perceived and experienced greater pressure to conform to stereotypes and had less favorable interactions with faculty and staff. Other studies indicate that students satisfied with campus life often persisted. Bennett and Okinaka (1990) found that Hispanic and white college students' attrition behavior and satisfaction with campus experiences correlated closely but differed for African Americans and Asian Americans. Their study revealed that as African American and Asian American students persisted to the fourth year of college, they appeared more dissatisfied with campus life than those African American and Asian American students who left prematurely.

Feagin and Sikes (1995) also found that greater social integration at a prominent PWI increased the probability of attrition for students of color. Conversely, Liu and Liu (2000) found that minority students did not have any greater tendency to be dissatisfied with the college environment than their white counterparts.

What the research suggests, therefore, is that although campus climate and campus satisfaction are important to many ethnic minority students' college retention, campus climate alone will not sustain high graduation and retention rates at colleges (Arrington 1994).

Special programmatic efforts, including bridge programs, structured campus residences, mentoring, and other ethnic and cultural programs designed to support ethnic minorities' academic and social integration, have eased some students' transition to college. These structured programs, however, tend to limit participating students' social and cultural networks to program experiences, which alienate them even further (Feagin and Sikes, 1995; Fiske, 1988; Himelhoch, Nichols, Ball, and Black, 1997).

Many PWIs want to create inclusive and safe learning environments that meet the needs of every student, but most higher education institutions must also adhere to constitutional law protecting freedom of speech. Although higher education institutions consider freedom of speech central to scholarly inquiry, they also recognize that this law and others inadvertently allow many perpetrators of biased and racist acts to go unpunished. According to a research report on campus codes of conduct, "As student populations become more diverse, it becomes more critical that administrators develop policies and programs conducive to campus learning environments where safety and civility will predominate" (Palmer, Penney, and Gehring, 1997, p. 118).

Actively supportive, nondiscriminatory campus environments are associated with greater college satisfaction, adjustment, and persistence. PWIs with successful minority graduation rates:

- Shift from tolerance to acceptance when minority enrollments reach a certain threshold
- Provide opportunities for cultural, social, and educational development to maintain a "comfortability factor"

- Examine and improve the institution's relationships with community minority organizations
- Commit institutional resources, such as visible leadership (including minority leadership) funds for educational intervention
- Employ a comprehensive and systemic approach
- Are supported by state legislation (Richardson, Simmons, and de los Santos, 1987)

PWIs have approached campus climate from programmatic and legal perspectives designed to ease ethnic minorities' college transition and protect their legal integrity. Yet Richardson and Skinner (1990) point out that although many PWIs address campus climate issues, they are hesitant about advocating systemic change because of the belief that campus diversity diminishes academic quality. The authors offer a model for diversity that harmoniously integrates access and achievement into the organizational culture through appropriate institutional goals and strategies. Ultimately, institutions that successfully support minority access and achievement focus on learning environment rather than race or ethnicity. Institutions that support diverse learning experiences are those that emphasize quality instruction and learning.

Commitment to Educational Goals and the Institution

Tinto (1993) hypothesized that commitment to occupational and educational goals (goal commitment) and commitment to the institution in which one enrolls (institutional commitment) significantly influence college performance and persistence (Okun, Benin, and Brandt-Williams, 1996). The stronger the goal commitment and institutional commitment, the more likely the student will graduate (Cabrera, Nora, and Castaneda, 1993). Tinto (1993) claims the scope of students' educational or occupational goals correlates positively with the probability of degree completion.

Astin's study investigating the relationship between career goals and student persistence (1977) found that students whose academic majors corresponded closely with their career goals were more likely to achieve their goals than were students with no identifiable career goal. In a subsequent study (1982), Astin concluded that career goals and intended academic majors were the strongest predictors of students' plans, suggesting that "the student's initial choice of a career or major is not a random event, and that it has considerable influence on the student's long-range career development" (p. 96). Pantages and Creedon (1978) also concluded that when students' values, goals, and attitudes correspond with those of their institution, the probability of graduation increases. In addition, the authors indicated that integration of a specific occupational goal into students' educational goals also increases their motivation and persistence.

The level of institutional commitment exhibited by a student depends on the congruence between the students' educational goals and the institution's mission. Although individuals may enter college with educational goals that are not commensurate with those of the institution, the level of congruence between student and institution is a primary factor influencing students' persistence. When undergraduates' educational goals are incongruent with those of the institution, the students are less likely to persist. Tinto (1975) notes that over time, goal and institutional commitment generally intensify as students clarify goals and focus on getting a degree.

Although literature examining goal and institutional commitment has been equivocal (Okun, Benin, and Brandt-Williams, 1996), research has shown that congruence between students' goals and institutional mission is mediated by academic and social components (Cabrera, Nora, and Castaneda, 1993). Tinto (1993) suggests that increased integration into academic and social campus communities causes greater institutional commitment and student persistence. One study (Beil, Resien, and Zea, 1999) confirmed that institutional commitment mediated the impact of students' first-semester academic and social integration on their persistence. The data seem to contradict previous findings indicating that academic and social integration have a direct impact on student retention. A student's integration into the campus determines that student's level of commitment to the institution, which directly influences decisions to persist. Kennedy, Sheckley, and Kehrhahn (2000) identified persisters as students who either improved their grade point averages over the course of the year, found their grade point averages to be consistent with their expectations, or adjusted academically to college. This research supports previous findings that students who integrate into the academic campus culture are more likely to persist. The research indicates that institutional practices should integrate students into the campus culture early and help them clarify career and academic goals through extensive and collaborative academic and career counseling.

Social and Academic Integration

Much of the literature regarding retention issues focuses on the social and academic integration of students with the university. Tinto's longitudinal model of student dropout (1975) posits that students' level of academic and social integration with the university (and their goal and institutional commitment) are the major factors in their ability to persist in college. Building on Durkheim's suicide theory, Tinto posits that, like suicide victims who were totally removed from the social fabric of society, students who are likewise removed from the social fabric of the college community are more likely to leave college than persist. "In Durkheim's view, individual integration into the social and intellectual life of society and the social and intellectual membership . . . that integration promotes are essential elements of social existence in human society. Societies with high rates of suicide are those whose social conditions are such as to constrain such membership" (Tinto, 1993, p. 102).

Tinto's theory suggests that students' ability to conform to or integrate into the social and intellectual membership of the university is pivotal to their ability to persevere through graduation. Griffen (1992), summarizing the attrition theories of Terenzini and Wright (1987), Spady (1970), Terenzini and Pascarella (1984), and Tinto (1975), further theorized that early integration into the social and academic fabric of the institution not only is correlated with persistence in college but also is conducive to the academic and social growth of the student. Rootman (1972) and Astin (1987) also subscribe to the theory of social and academic integration but suggest that the important issue to be considered is the student's environmental fit into the social confines of the institution. How a student's values fit in with the institutional values and those of the faculty and student population will affect the quality of that relationship.

Students actually fit into the college environment in a variety of ways, and the college can assist in that integration in a number of ways. The development of new friendships and peer interaction are perhaps the most recognized methods of social integration. This development can help students bridge the often traumatic first weeks of the freshman year and offer other areas of personal and academic support. Several studies, including those conducted by Tinto (1975), Pantages and Creedon (1978), and Astin (1977), have found that friendship support is directly related to persistence in college and that college dropouts perceive themselves as having less social interaction than those students who persist in college. For African American students, students who engage in social activities become a part of the social environment and are more likely to persist (Griffen, 1992).

The process of becoming socially integrated into the fabric of the university has also been found to be both a cumulative and compounding process. Terenzini and Wright (1987) suggest that the level of social integration during a given year of study is part of a cumulative experience that continues to build throughout one's college experience. Therefore, the experiences that a student encounters in his freshman year will influence and support integration in subsequent years.

HBCUs have also been found to provide more positive social support for African American students than PWIs offer. Berg and Peplau (1982) concluded that African American students on black campuses exhibited fewer adjustment problems, engaged in more social activities through their student networking, had higher GPAs, exhibited greater satisfaction in their college experience, and had higher occupational expectations than their counterparts at PWIs.

The establishment of peer relations during college also supports a student's academic integration into the university. Capella, Hetzler, and MacKenzie (1983) found that a positive peer influence favorably influenced the study habits of college students. Several studies, including a 1983 study of exemplary precollege science, engineering, mathematics, and computer science intervention programs for female and minority students, concluded that peer relationships were important in keeping students interested in the sciences (Matyas, 1991; Malcom, 1983). Many intervention programs build upon this theory of peer support, including the University of California, Berkeley's Mathematics Workshop Program, Xavier's Project SOAR, and the University of California, San Diego's Summer Bridge Program, all of which encourage group interaction and peer integration.

The development of role models and mentors has also been defined in the literature as important factors in student integration, both academically and socially. A positive role model provides students with a number of equally positive experiences. The availability of role models extends beyond the social integration of the student: "It is not surprising that a number of studies have found that social interaction with the college's faculty is related to persistence in college. Spady (1971) suggested that these findings arise from the fact that interaction with the faculty not only increases social integration and therefore institutional commitment but also increases the individual's academic integration" (Tinto, 1993, p. 109).

On the college campus, faculty members are often role models. The interaction between faculty and students has been identified as a major factor in the ability of students to persist in college while also increasing their level of satisfaction (Astin, 1977; Beal and Noel, 1980; Pascarella and Terenzini, 1979). Positive role models provide guidance, direction, and, most important, a good example for students to learn from. Interaction between faculty and students outside class is even more beneficial to students. Informal contact between students and faculty members has been found to increase the persistence of the student (Ugbah and Williams, 1989; Griffen, 1992; Astin, 1982). Endo and Harpel (1982) concluded that informal contact with faculty was a foundation for the development of friendly relationships between students and faculty that had a positive influence on students in terms of their personal, social, and intellectual development (Griffen, 1992). Terenzini and Pascarella (1977, 1980) had similar findings but were unable to duplicate the outcomes at another campus, concluding that each individual campus may react differently to the interactions of variables (Pascarella, 1984).

With regard to underrepresented minorities in universities, contact with positive role models is even more significant than it is for majority students. A study of a mentoring program at Ohio University in Athens, Ohio, found that 91 percent of the African American protégés felt more confident as a result of their mentor (Ugbah and Williams, 1989).

National statistics confirm the scarcity of minority role models on campus. African Americans, Hispanics, and American Indians are substantially underrepresented among faculty at colleges and universities relative to their representation among students. Analyses of data from the IPEDS Fall Staff Survey show that only 8 percent of all full-time faculty at four-year colleges and universities nationwide in fall 1997 were black, Hispanic, or American Indian/Alaskan Native. Moreover, a substantial share of minority faculty are employed at minority-serving institutions. For example, African Americans represent 59 percent of all full-time faculty at HBCUs but only 3 percent of all full-time faculty at four-year non-HBCUs.

Minorities are even more severely underrepresented among tenured faculty. Only 7 percent of full-time tenured faculty who were employed at four-year colleges and universities in 1997 were African American, Hispanic, or American Indian (analyses of IPEDS 1997 Fall Staff Survey). Again, including minority-serving institutions in the analyses masks the magnitude of the underrpresentation of minorities among faculty at PWIs. African Americans held only 2 percent of the full-time, tenured faculty positions at four-year, non-HBCUs nationwide in fall 1997.

Even among administrators, deficient minority representation is evident. Analyses of data from the IPEDS Fall Staff Survey show that African Americans, Hispanics, and American Indians held 12 percent of all full-time executive, administrative, and managerial positions at four-year colleges and universities in fall 1997. Excluding employment at HBCUs reduces the representation of African Americans, Hispanics, and American Indians among top administrators at four-year institutions to 10 percent.

As Franklin (1988) notes, the lack of positive role models, advocates, and mentors has an impact on students and their ability to do well in elementary and secondary schools. Moreover, the risk of minority students leaving school is much higher. Therefore, informal contact between faculty and students is more critical than ever, and institutions must work diligently to provide positive faculty role models for their students (Justiz, 1994). Successful academic and social integration is also more likely for students who live on campus. Several studies have shown the positive effects of on-campus residence (Pascarella, 1984; Chickering, 1974; Astin, 1977; Pantages and Creedon,

1978). Pascarella (1984) found that even when background traits and institutional controls were held constant, on-campus living was positively correlated with higher student interaction, although he was not able to significantly determine the academic affects. Astin (1977) also found a greater interaction with faculty and peers and that students were more satisfied with college, had more focused career and educational goals, and in turn were more likely to persist to graduation.

Financial Aid

Economic theory and educational research suggest that for students to persist to a college degree, the returns for receiving the degree must outweigh the costs (over time) of attaining it. Because attending college has direct, indirect, and opportunity costs for students, financing decisions have both short- and long-term effects on college persistence.

For most students, decisions about enrollment and persistence are driven by labor market returns for receiving a degree. Most research suggests that attending college and persisting to degree completion will be rewarded with higher annual and lifetime earnings. In 1998, for instance, the median annual earnings for men age 25 and older and employed full time was $31,477 for those with a high school diploma, $40,274 for an associate's degree, $51,405 for a bachelor's degree, $64,244 for a master's degree, $75,078 for a doctoral degree, and $94,737 for a first professional degree (U.S. Department of Education, 2001b). Persisting in college has other rewards, of course; for example, degree holders participate to a greater extent in voting and other civic responsibilities (Institute for Higher Education Policy, 1998). But for most students to persist—particularly low-income and minority students—the benefits of attaining a degree usually must be greater than the direct, indirect, and opportunity costs required to attend an institution.

For many low-income and minority students, enrollment and persistence are driven by the availability of financial aid. In 2001, the median household income of African American families headed by a householder age 45 to 54 (the families most likely to have traditional college-age children) was $36,824, and $41,652 for Hispanics. By comparison, white households had a combined income of $61,643 (U.S. Census Bureau, 2001). Thus, by definition, more

African American and Latino families will require financial assistance to attend and persist in college.

Students from low-income families were more likely to receive grant aid to attend college. In 1999–00, 77 percent of financially dependent students from families with less than $20,000 in family income received some financial aid, with an average award of $6,727. In contrast, 44 percent of those from families with income of $100,000 or more received aid, with an average award of $7,838 (higher-income students received higher average awards because they tended to be enrolled at higher-cost institutions). Once in college, three-quarters of the low-income undergraduates received grant aid, with an average award of $4,309, compared with 29 percent of higher-income students who received grants, with an average award of $5,100 (U.S. Department of Education, 2001c).

Even with the availability of financial aid, however, students from racial and ethnic minorities and low-income families are less likely than whites and those from higher-income families to enroll in a four-year college and earn bachelor's degree (Advisory Committee on Student Financial Assistance, 2001; Gladieux and Swail, 1998; Thayer, 2000). More than one-half of African American, Hispanic, and Native American dependent students come from families with incomes of less than $30,000 (King, 1999). In 1999, the most recent year of available data, about 57 percent of high school graduates from families in the lowest-income quartile entered college, compared with nearly 86 percent of those from the highest-income quartile. Even more troubling is the fact that the percentage of low-income students who completed college by age 24 has remained at less than 10 percent for the past thirty years, while the percentage of students from the highest-income families who received bachelor's degrees rose from 40 percent to about 60 percent (Mortenson, 2001a, 2001c).

Recent Financial Aid Policy Developments.   Recent financial aid policy developments have led to disparities between the availability of grant and loan aid (Advisory Committee on Student Financial Assistance, 2001; Christman, 2000; Mortenson, 2001b; Thayer, 2000). According to the College Board, the proportion of financial aid from grants has declined from about 50 percent in

1990–91 to 40 percent in 2000–01 (College Board, 2001b). A series of federal financial aid policies created during the 1980s and 1990s led to this shift in grant and loan aid availability:

The reduced purchasing power of need-based grants, relative to increases in college costs. In inflation-adjusted value, appropriations for federal Pell Grants grew by 23 percent over the last decade, but tuition and fee charges at four-year public colleges and universities rose by 40 percent (College Board, 2001b; American Council on Education, 2000; Cunningham and O'Brien, 1999).

More grant aid has come from state and institutional sources than the federal government (Cunningham and O'Brien, 1999). In recent years, funding for institutional and state grants has grown by more than 90 percent, while federal grant aid grew just 31 percent.

The shift in federal aid to student loans and tax credits. Federal student loan volume grew from $17.1 billion in 1990–91 to $37.1 billion in 2000–01. Much of this growth occurred in the federal Stafford Unsubsidized Loan program, which jumped 50 percent since 1995–96. Additionally, under the Taxpayer Relief Act of 1997, students will be eligible for more than $40 billion in tax credits (through the Hope Scholarship Tax Credit and the Lifetime Learning Tax Credit) over the next decade to pay for college (Reindl and Redd, 1998). Because low-income students are less likely to have tax liability, they are less likely to benefit from these new federal tax credits (Reindl and Redd, 1998).

Shift of institutional and state grant aid from need-based to merit-based criteria. During the 1990s, more states and institutions began to use more of their grant funds to award merit and other nonneed-based aid (Heller, 1999; Reindl and Redd, 1998). Institutions used more merit aid to entice more students with high SAT scores and other characteristics to enroll on their campuses. Some states, particularly those in the South, reacted to the concerns of middle- and upper-income families who did not qualify for Pell Grants and other awards that are distributed based on families' demonstrated financial need but wanted additional funds to send their children to college. Institutional and state funding for merit and other nonneed grants nearly doubled during the early and mid-1990s, while need-based aid grew by 30 percent and 41 percent in the same periods. These nonneed awards tend to favor students from middle- and upper-income families; during the 1990s, Heller (1999) points out, the number of low-income students who received nonneed grants at private colleges and universities fell 10 percent, while the number of awards to high-income students grew 24 percent.

Fundamentally, these policy shifts mean that relatively more low-income students will have to borrow to enroll in college and persist to a degree. Prior research and anecdotal evidence has suggested that low-income students and minority students are much less willing to borrow to attend college than whites or students from higher-income families (Olivas, 1985; Mortenson and Wu, 1990). Recent data indicate that Pell Grant recipients, who are often low-income, first-generation students, are more likely to borrow than are students who do not receive Pell Grants. These students tend to graduate with an average debt 30 percent greater than students receiving other types of financial aid (American Council on Education, 2000). Thus, the shift from grants to loans may have implications for persistence levels of low-income and minority students.

Financial Aid and Persistence. In light of these recent policy developments, it is important to understand the linkages between financial aid, enrollment, and persistence for students in general and racial and ethnic minority students in particular. Fortunately, research on these questions is abundant. Some of these prior researchers (Bean, 1986; Metzner and Bean, 1987; Cabrera, Castaneda, Nora, and Hengstler, 1992; Cabrera, Nora, and Castaneda, 1992) suggest that students' ability to pay for college consists of two dimensions: an objective component, reflecting students' availability of resources, and a subjective component, reflecting students' perceptions of their capacity to or difficulty in financing a college education. It is likely that these factors also influence students' decisions about college choice and persistence.

Further research (Mumper, 1996; St. John, Paulsen, and Starkey, 1996; St. John and Starkey, 1995) measures students' response to a set of prices rather than a single price; it found that students with different needs respond to tuition and financial aid quite differently. Therefore, different combinations of tuition and student aid yield different levels of enrollment and persistence. Price choices are influenced by type of institution, attendance status, and residence status. Students are also influenced by type of aid (grants, loans, work-study, other) in their aid packages. Further, low-income students have been found to be more responsive to tuition increases than are middle- and upper-income students (Heller, 2001a).

Yet the research investigating the effects of the types, amounts, and combinations of financial aid on college persistence is, at best, ambivalent. This ambivalence shows direct and indirect influences on persistence and reflects the financial aid policies of the period studied (Fenske, Porter, and DuBrock, 2000; Heller, 2001b; Murdock, 1990; Perna, 1998). Earlier research in this area found financial aid to be unrelated to college students' persistence (Moline, 1987; Peng and Fetters, 1978), but more recent findings indicate its importance to the recruitment and retention of low-income students (Murdock, 1990; St. John, Kirshstein, and Noel (1991)). Recent path analyses, on the other hand, have indicated that the receipt of financial aid has only marginal effects on students' persistence and completion. Receiving financial aid and the amount received ranked eighth among total effects on persistence (Perna, 1998).

Persistence by Race or Ethnicity and Grants Versus Loans. Such findings vary by type of aid received and the time period under study. Need-based institutional grants tend to facilitate persistence (Fenske, Porter, and DuBrock, 2000; Murdock, 1990; Pantages and Creedon, 1978; Porter, 1989). Porter (1989), for instance, found that 90 percent of students who received grants in their first year, regardless of race or ethnicity or type of institution, were still enrolled in the second semester. Meanwhile, the persistence rate of students who did not receive grant aid was 75 percent overall and 60 percent for African American students. Further, the highest completion rates were associated with aid limited to grants and packages consisting of grants, loans, and work-study. Completion rates were lower for students whose packages emphasized loans (Murdock, 1990; Perna, 1998, St. John, Kirshstein, and Noel, 1991). These disparities were even more evident in the 1970s, when a higher proportion of aid came from grants and persistence rates between nonwhite and white students were equal after controlling for receipt of aid and other factors (St. John, Kirshstein, and Noel, 1991). Blanchette (1994) used the High School and Beyond data set to conclude that additional grant aid increased graduation rates for some minority students.

Loans, however, may not be as effective in retaining low-income or minority students. Some studies have concluded loan aid is unrelated to persistence, while others have found students who receive loan aid are less likely to persist. Student background tends to influence the effect of loan aid on persistence. For example, loans have been found to be less consistent in facilitating access for minority students than for white students (St. John, 1991). Other research (Blanchette, 1994) found that a $1,000 increase in loan aid would increase the probability of dropping out for African American students but that for Hispanic students the probability is slightly lower. Although Ekstrom (1991) found that students who were willing to accumulate debt to finance college enrollments were more likely to persist, other research (Olivas, 1985; Mortenson and Wu, 1990) demonstrated that African American and Hispanic students were less willing to finance their education with loans than were their white counterparts.

College employment also appears to have an influence on persistence (Horn, 1998; Pascarella and others, 1994). The type and extent of influence of employment on student outcomes depend on the number of employment hours, location of employment, and the degree to which the student's job is related to his or her academic or career goals. Horn and Maw (1994) found that although receipt of financial aid had little effect on whether students worked or did not work, it did influence the number of hours that students decided to work. Undergraduates who received higher amounts of student aid were less likely to work full time than those who received lesser amounts of student aid. Likewise, students with higher net education costs were more likely to work and work full time than undergraduates with lower net costs. Students who worked fifteen hours or fewer per week were more likely to have high academic grade point averages than were those who worked more hours.

The federal work-study program, which provides part-time jobs to financially needy postsecondary education students, has been found to increase student persistence, but external employment (non-work-study) through full-time and off-campus employment tends to decrease students' persistence, unless related to area of study (Horn and Maw, 1994).

These research findings suggest that a link exists between receipt of financial aid—particularly grant aid—and persistence. Low-income and minority students who receive grants generally are more likely to persist than those who receive loans. Given the rising costs of attending college, however, it is unlikely that low-income students will be able to receive bachelor's degrees without *any* loan aid. The key may be in educating these students in strategies for borrowing wisely, that is, borrowing only what is truly needed to persist in college. Many of the students who have trouble with debt are those who borrow beyond their financial need (King 1999). At the same time, the research also suggests that the shifts in aid from grants to loans and from need- to merit-based programs adversely affect both enrollment and persistence for minority students. Reversing these shifts may be necessary to increase college access and success for low-income and minority students.

A Framework for Retention

A S DISCUSSED IN THE PREVIOUS CHAPTER, a number of theories and models have been developed to explain student attrition in
higher education. In particular, Tinto's attrition model (1975), Bean's synthetic model (1982), and Anderson's force field analysis (1985) are among
those theories that attempt to describe and categorize the attrition process.
Like all theories, however, these models are open for interpretation and,
depending on a number of variables and constructs, cannot be used to describe
all peoples, organizations, and situations.

A New Perspective on Student Integration

Although these models are very useful in illustrating the problems and
processes relating to student persistence, lost between the simplicity and complexity of the different models is the relationship between college and student.
Without a clear explanation of what the model represents, it is difficult for
administrators and practitioners to fully comprehend the significance of
the model and how it relates to campus policy. Introduced here is a geometric model of student persistence and achievement that focuses on students'
attributes and institutional practice. The model simultaneously describes persistence and achievement because of the inextricable relationship between the
two variables. For example, the intervention of a motivational instructor may
not only prompt certain students to persist but also cause them to study more
and likely score better on exams and assignments.

The geometric model differs from others by placing the student at the center of the model rather than making him or her an indifferent element in a flow chart or structural equation model. As Tinto (2000) commented, none of the models discuss the connection between classroom and retention, the one place where the institution has the closest connection to the student. The same can be said for how the models address students.

The purpose of this model is to provide a user-friendly method for discussion and to focus on the cognitive and social attributes that the student brings to campus, and the institutional role in the student experience. The ultimate question is simple: What can an institution do to help each student get through college? And how can institutions help integrate students academically and socially into the campus, as well as support their cognitive and social development? The three sides of the model shown in Figure 17 each represent a particular force on a student, represented by the area inside the triangle. Similar to Anderson's force field analysis, the triangle represents the complex set of internal processes within each student that foster his or her ability to persist and achieve. The area external to the triangle represents all outside variables impacting on the student's development and decision making.

FIGURE 17
Swail's Geometric Model of Student Persistence and Achievement

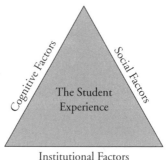

Institutional Factors

Three Forces Affecting Student Persistence and Achievement

In terms of college persistence and achievement, three particular forces account for the entire spectrum of student outcomes: cognitive, social, and institutional factors (see Figure 18). Briefly stated, the cognitive factors form the academic ability—the strengths and weaknesses—of the student, such as the level of proficiency in reading, writing, and mathematics. Social factors, such as the ability to interact effectively with other persons, personal attitudes, and cultural history, form a second set of external factors that characterize the individual. The third set of factors, institutional, refers to the practices, strategies, and culture of the college or university that, in either an intended or unintended way, impact student persistence and achievement. Examples include faculty teaching ability, academic support programming, financial aid, student services, recruitment and admissions, academic services, and curriculum and instruction. (They are described more completely later in this section.)

FIGURE 18
Forces Acting on the Geometric Model of Student Persistence and Achievement

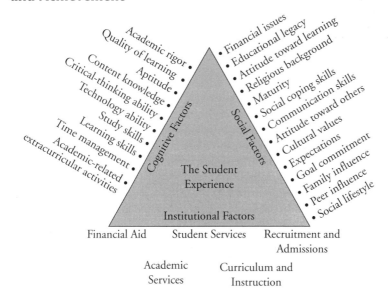

Cognitive Factors

The cognitive factors relate to the intelligence,[3] knowledge, and academic ability a student brings with him or her to the college environment. These factors may be measured by such variables as course selection and completion in high school, aptitude, or extracurricular involvement in academic-related areas. Cognitive factors are important because they directly relate to the student's ability to comprehend and complete the academic portion of the college curriculum.

An important element of the cognitive factors relating to student persistence and achievement is the student's decision-making and problem-solving ability. The decision-making process is an important part of the models described earlier. Tinto (1975, 1993) describes the decision-making process regarding goal commitment and dropout, Bean (1982) describes an intent to leave, and Anderson (1985) identifies value conflicts and career indecision among the important variables that a student controls through the set of social and cultural values instilled in him or her. The student's decision-making process occurs within the confines of the geometric shape represented in the model presented above. It is here that the social and cognitive factors interconnect to form the decision-making process.

Social Factors

The second factor related to student persistence and performance is the set of social factors impacting on students. Such factors include parental and peer support, the development or existence of career goals, educational legacy, and the ability to cope in social situations. The social issues facing college students are of ever-increasing interest to higher education personnel. The research field generally agrees about the importance of social integration with regard to student retention and the fact that students have a difficult time persisting when they are not socially integrated into campus life. Thus, the factors identified on the social side of the geometric model are uniquely important to students' stability.

A student's social underpinning and opportunities have obviously crossover impact on his or her cognitive development. A student who is brought up in

[3]Intelligence is meant in the form akin to Gardner's multiple intelligence theory, where it is not just an academic sense of intelligence but the intellectual ability of an individual to work through many different mediums, such as music.

a culturally and educationally rich environment will develop skills critical to postsecondary, career, and personal success. Students hailing from less supportive environments may bring with them deficiencies in their self-esteem and efficacy, especially as they relate to academics when compared with students from more advantaged backgrounds.

Institutional Factors

College is undoubtedly the biggest social change a traditional-age student has ever undertaken. College presents stresses, at some level, to all students. Substantial research exists on the stresses of freshman year, especially on minority and low-income students. Regardless of one's subscription to either Gennep's social anthropology theory (Tinto, 1988) or to Valentine's biculturation theory (Rendón, Jalomo, and Nora, 2000; Valentine, 1971), how the institution reacts to students is of primary importance to retention, persistence, and completion.

The institutional side of the triangle relates to the ability of the institution to provide appropriate support to students during the college years, both academically and socially. Issues related to course availability, content, and instruction affect a student's ability to persist, as do support mechanisms such as tutoring, mentoring, and career counseling. Although this axis has a direct effect on a student's stability during college, it also can be seen as a flexible set of programs or conditions that the college can mold to meet the diverse needs and attributes of individual students.

The significance of setting institutional factors on equal ground with cognitive and social factors is to illustrate the importance of campus participation and knowledge in students' social and academic development. The geometric model places this set of factors at the base of the triangle because it is the college that forms the foundation for college success. It is here that the institution can identify and match the needs of individual students, a student cohort group, or the student body as a whole.

The Model in Practice

The strength of the geometric model is that it allows users to move from a theoretical conversation to a study of practice in the present and over time. On the theoretical level, using the geometric nature of this model helps us understand persistence, how various factors may interact, and how the institution is involved in the persistence process. Only through the collection of data to further understand the cognitive and social experiences of students can the institution know how to act on these theoretical structures. Thus, we begin with the theoretical and move toward the practical, starting with a discussion of equilibrium.

Achieving Equilibrium

The geometric model allows us to discuss the dynamics between cognitive, social, and institutional factors, all of which take place within the student. We use the word *equilibrium* to define the status of a student when he or she is in a mode to persist in college. That is, the forces of cognitive, social, and institutional factors must combine from some type of equilibrium, or balance, to provide a solid foundation for student growth, development, and persistence. When equilibrium is lost, students risk reducing their academic and social integration with the institution and therefore risk stopping or dropping out (Spady, 1970; Tinto, 1975). This process is described in the following paragraphs.

Stage One. Each side of the geometric model represents a series of variables that define the cognitive, social, and institutional structure of the student experience. Each variable, in its own right, has an impact on the persistence process. In fact, each variable has one of three consequences for the student: it can positively, negatively, or neutrally impact student persistence and growth. As illustrated in Figure 19, the net result is a series of plus and minus

FIGURE 19
Impact of Individual Factors or Attributes on Student Persistence and Achievement

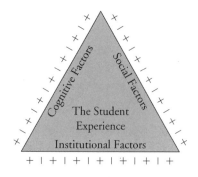

experiences that mold the behavior and characteristics of the student. It is important to note that each force or impact on the student is distinct and different. Thus, one should not infer that the effect of one variable can be equally neutralized by another. It is reasonable to assume, however, that certain variables can alter the effect of other variables. Thus, the individual impact of variables can combine and work with or against other variables, known as *reciprocity*. If we could algebraically calculate the impact of these variables, we would end up with a *beta value* to describe the cognitive, social, and institutional value. Although theoretically possible, it would be a massively challenging practice to equate all inputs to a singular coefficient.

An example of reciprocity is the combination of academic motivation, appropriate learning environments, and academic support. The net effect of these three variables (and surely dozens of others) could have a dramatic effect on student achievement and ultimately persistence in college. This combination of forces—the reciprocity of variables effect—gives us a net effect for each of the three planes of the geometric model.

Stage Two. The second stage refers to the continuation of our reciprocity theory to the entire spectrum of variable interaction, that is, between cognitive, social, and institutional variables. The force generated by all variables—either individually or across axes—accounts for the stability or instability of student persistence and achievement and ultimately the achievement of equilibrium.

Although balance may be achieved on each axis of the triangle (as shown in the prior figures), it is naive to suggest that an equal balance exists among the three sides of the model, even if we could define what that balance would look like. In other words, rarely would the triangle be truly equilateral. The complexity of human behavior and learning theory suggests that there is an infinite combination of variables from each of the three axes that can result in an outcome measurable through student persistence and achievement. As previously stated, however, we use the word *equilibrium* to define the status when the cognitive, social, and institutional forces combine in a manner that supports student persistence and achievement—that is, the model is stable and supports persistence and achievement.

Moreover, a seemingly perfect, equilateral polygon (that is, equal effect from each resource) does not necessarily constitute the best model of stability for a student. Not only is this effect seemingly impossible, but it is illogical to assume that an equilateral model is a reasonable description of human ability and behavior. Rather, the individuality of the student necessitates that the model must shift and sway and evolve in a variety of ways and still provide a model of stability. The human condition is very much an ebb-and-flow, far-from-static situation, where shifts in one social or cognitive area prompt a protective response to counterbalance that shift. To illustrate this point, Figure 20 introduces four variations of model stability, all of which are in a state of equilibrium, therefore supporting student persistence. Illustration A represents the so-called "perfect" situation where the student has relatively equivalent levels of cognitive and social resources and requires a similar level of institutional commitment to aid his or her persistence and performance. The bar chart to the side of the illustration helps to define the relative force of each axis apart from the illustration. In this case, the three levels, cognitive, social, and institutional, are similar.

Illustration B represents a student with low academic resources but excellent social skills, with the requisite institutional intervention and support. Through social networks, strong will, and the appropriate assistance from the institution, the student may be able to apply the necessary cognitive skills while also developing new skills to succeed in college. An example is a good-natured student who lacks the academic fortitude, perhaps because of a below-average education during middle and high school. With diagnosis from the institution and the implementation of appropriate support programs, the student could persist in college and build up his or her cognitive resources.

Illustration C represents a student with high cognitive resources and low social resources. The cognitive ability of the student is so strong that even the institutional forces are below average level. A person who may fit this model could be the stereotypical brilliant thinker whose social skills leave something to be desired. In most cases, we would think that this type of student will persist to graduation, but because the college experience is about more than completion and about developing the individual to his or her full social and academic potential, it is important for the institution to consider interventions

FIGURE 20
Variations on Model Stability

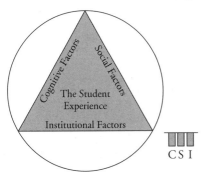

A. The Perfect Polygon. *The three forces exert essentially the same presence or level of force, such that the cognitive and social attributes of the student are supported equally by the institution.*

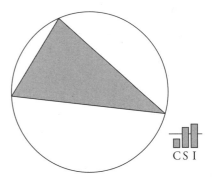

B. Socially Strong/Academically Weak. *In this scenario, the student has weak cognitive/academic skills but very strong social skills. The institution must match the academic needs of the student to achieve equilibrium.*

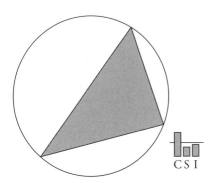

C. Cognitively Strong/Socially Weak. *The student has very strong cognitive/academic skills but is low on the social scale. Thus, the institution must provide social stimulation and situations to integrate the student into the campus community.*

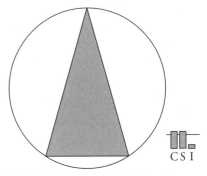

D. Socially and Cognitively Strong. *This student is gifted in academics and social skills. In some ways, the institution just needs to "be there," and not get in the way. Only a catastrophic event will push this student off the completion track.*

to help that student develop social skills that will be beneficial throughout his or her life.

The last example, D, illustrates a student with extremely high cognitive and social ability, therefore negating much of the need for institutional support beyond those related to basic instruction. In fact, it is likely that the institution acts more as a barrier than a conduit to goal attainment for students fitting this mold. With such strong academic and social skills plus related resources, these students probably tear through the curriculum (the classic distance education student).

As described, the graphic representations in Figure 20 illustrate four different student models; all are considered in equilibrium because of the ability of the institution to deliver the appropriate level of support services to counter the strengths and weaknesses of the student. If one component of the model is forced to overcompensate for too many negative factors attributed to the other two sides of the triangle, then the student is likely to run into problems. Thus, a student with low net cognitive resources and low net social resources is unlikely to persist in college, regardless of what the institution may provide in terms of support services.

A Chronological Metric

The model can also be used to represent the cognitive and social growth of students over time. Figure 21 illustrates the time element, where the triangle represents the present and the area beyond the triangle represents all prior influences and experiences, as recent as yesterday, as far back as preschool, if necessary. This concept is especially important at the time of college matriculation, for it can provide college administrators, faculty, and staff a snapshot of a student's cognitive and social attributes at the entry point into college. Given that the triangle sides represent the present, the institution must have a process for identifying the impacts and abilities of the student beyond the triangle, that is, measuring their capabilities based on their progress during the K–12 years. Colleges typically use standardized test scores, GPAs, course transcripts, and even support letters and interviews to gauge a student's past.

For the institution, the ability to learn about a student's history is more than about testing and analysis. It is an opportunity to connect with the student and become cognizant of his or her goals and aspirations. With this information, the institution can modify individual programs to meet specific needs of the student. The entire admissions process allows an institution the opportunity to match its goals with those of the student.

FIGURE 21
**Time as a Variable on the Geometric Model of Student
Persistence and Achievement**

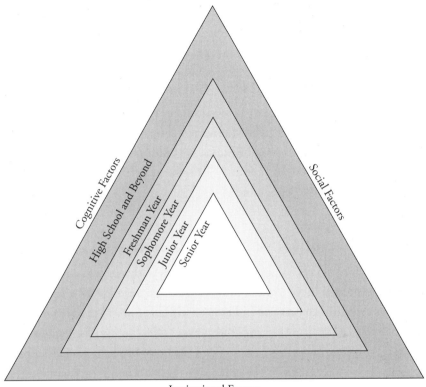

Institutional Factors

Of course, time does not hold still during the college years. In fact, the college experience represents the coming of age and entrance into adulthood for most traditional-age students. Therefore, it is important for the institution to note that the student's goals, aspirations, and abilities change during his or her time on campus and that strategies identified by the student must be matched by subsequent changes on the part of the institution.

As can be seen in the figure, the geometric model can be used to conceptually track a student's progression through graduation. Remembering that the innermost triangle represents the here and now and that every piece of time that passes moves farther outward from the center we can thus layer each progressive period of time as it occurs. From a theoretical point of view, the model has the ability to consider all prior history, including high school and beyond. From a practical point of view, it can help us gather and use information chronologically to chart or track students' progress before matriculation and during college. This observation is significant, because it gives us a philosophical picture of how students progress and change over time. For an institution, it can provide the necessary knowledge and information to gauge institutional practices and alter the individual learning plans associated with each student. For example, on the social side of the model, an institution can and should track the student's social development, as measured through appropriate inventories administered biannually or annually. Likewise, the academic progression of the student can be measured through credits earned, course grades, and course examinations.

Practical Implications of the Geometric Model

The strength of the geometric model introduced in this paper lies in the snapshot it can provide administrators and practitioners regarding the relationship between institutional practice and the academic and social needs of the campus population. If the institution is to support these needs, it is necessary that they identify and understand them. Just because a particular student population has previously exhibited certain tendencies through its academic ability does not assure an institution that all students will represent that behavior. Therefore, the institution must base its policy decision making on a continual assessment of individual student needs.

Tinto (1993), Pantages and Creedon (1978), and others have suggested the importance of institutional and student fit with regard to persistence. It is often the incongruence between institutional goals and student goals that leads to students' dropping out (Tinto, 1975). The nature of the person-environment fit theory also explains these phenomena. Differences between the commitment of students to the institution and the institution to the student may well define the comfort level of the student in terms of persistence. Part of the human condition is the need to comfort and be comforted, and institutions must provide a culture that supports these values. It is through the matching of student goals and attributes and institutional mission that a positive state of equilibrium can be developed.

This model works to help describe the persistence process and the delicate balance between student resources (for example, what the student brings to campus) and institutional resources (for example, what the institution provides for the student). But the strength in the model and the framework that follows is in its ability to help institutions work proactively to support student persistence and achievement. For instance, if the institution has requisite knowledge of individual student background and goals, it can then provide a menu of programs and support opportunities to make up for any social or academic deficiencies. Most college diagnosis is limited to the collection of SAT scores, high school GPA, and course grades, which is far from exhaustive in terms of understanding the student persona. In fact, they provide a unidimensional perspective of the student. Very little is done to observe students' affective and social talents or challenges, which are important components of the persistence puzzle. Furthermore, the standard diagnostics do not account for any "intelligences" other than the mathematical-rational. Institutions should collect data to provide administrators and faculty with a more concise picture of the student body. The more understanding the institution is of students' needs, the better prepared it is to design and implement programs and support services to meet those needs. Many colleges are now using diagnostic assessments before matriculation to ascertain students' level of academic ability. The next step would be to begin to ask questions regarding students' social development and preparedness.

Let us first ask what type of data is representative of our needs. Beyond that of academic scores or ranking, institutions could develop an entirely different process for recruiting and admitting students (Guinier, 2001). The process might include the development of a portfolio of student work that covers his or her entire high school experience, including art, music, physics, languages, and even extracurricular activities. The interest and involvement of a student in the Young Astronauts Club or the Technology Student Association may be just as compelling as a physics grade, because they illustrate the student's desire, motivation, and development of knowledge within a particular discipline.

The institution might also require statements from teachers about the nature of the student, much like a letter of reference for a job application. At a certain stage, colleges should interview students and get to know them on a personal level, where appropriate. Although some colleges do so, it is not a widespread practice, especially at large campuses. The formation of precollege outreach programs can bring students closer to the college, metaphorically speaking. Alumni clubs, recent graduates, and undergraduate and graduate students can all be used as intermediaries in recruiting students.

Diagnostic and supplementary knowledge of the student is a vital component of the geometric model. Without this knowledge, the institution is incapable of making prudent decisions about whom to admit. In fact, this process is bidirectional, because the initial phase of getting to know the student is also the stage where the student gets to know the institution, and only through this information sharing can either party effectively assess the fit between them.

It is also reasonable to assume that through the college experience, students change, both cognitively and socially. As Tinto (1982) states, "We have reasons to believe that the forces that lead to dropout in the early stages of the academic career can be quite different from those that influence dropout later" (p. 693). Therefore, institutions must provide support at each step of the process, not just during the freshman year.

A Framework for Student Retention

Most frameworks or "models" focus on departure and the paths through postsecondary education. In this chapter, we introduce a framework focused on student retention and success.

Purpose of the Framework

The campus-wide retention framework that follows was designed to provide administrators with a strategy and framework to build a student retention program that incorporates the individual needs of its students and the institution. It was designed with the hope that this framework will allow administrators and planners to devote more of their time to planning and management rather than to the uncovering of research to support their actions. It is a most important provision, as the literature is often equivocal. That is, the sheer complexity of student retention and the plethora of factors that impact students before and during college make it difficult to assess the final meaning of the aggregate research available on retention. We hope this framework helps ameliorate that problem.

With respect to program development and operation, an important aspect of the framework is the identification of organizational strategies that best support the planning and implementation of the student retention program. Regardless of the knowledge acquired and assessed by the institution, the need to follow a practical course of planning and implementation is essential to the ultimate success of any endeavor. Thus, the identification of successful organizational and planning strategies is imperative to this study and to institutions interested in fostering systemic change. They are discussed in the next chapter.

From an administrative perspective, the strategies introduced in the framework are not prescriptive. They are applied as examples of institutional practices that are consistent with current thinking within the various communities as well as what we have been able to ascertain through research.

Finally, this framework will be particularly significant in providing an understanding of the various roles that will be expected and required of administrators, faculty members, and staff members on campus if the effort is to be successful.

The genesis of this research framework was a doctoral research study by Swail (1995), which focused on minority student retention in science, engineering, and mathematics. Swail's study was based on an extensive review of pertinent literature, which resulted in the development of a series of research-based institutional practices that had been shown to effectively increase minority student persistence. They were placed into five categories: student services, academic services, curriculum and instruction, recruitment and admissions, and financial aid.

The second stage of Swail's research (1995) involved the formation of a national panel of experts and scholars in the area of minority student persistence. Based on nominations from established scholars and practitioners, sixteen experts—including vice presidents of educational foundations, senior scholars at national associations, and nationally recognized researchers and professors—were selected to participate. Participating in a two-stage Delphi technique, the panel responded to the five-category framework.

The first Delphi round formed the foundation of the study by allowing panelists to comment on the five-category framework. Panelists were asked to rate individual objectives of the framework on a four-point Likert-type scale and add comments regarding each objective. After the responses were analyzed, a second round focused on ranking and clarifying the objectives within the framework.

Panelists were asked to comment on and modify the framework based on their specific expertise and experience. The result of this two-stage Delphi inquiry was a research-based framework that outlines a series of practices that may help reduce student attrition in science, engineering, and mathematics.

Since that study, a number of pertinent research studies have been conducted and the importance of student retention has once again been recognized. Based on subsequent literature reviews and research, it was believed that the framework could easily be modified to encompass other disciplines beyond science, engineering, and mathematics.

A Research-Based Framework

Studies and issues regarding minority student persistence are not new, and many of the practices identified and outlined in this research-based framework have been presented before. Two main differences between this framework and previous efforts include the broad scope of coverage across a variety of campus issues and the specific recommendations for institutional practice. The framework provides administrators and practitioners with a menu of activities, policies, and practices to consider during the planning and implementation of a comprehensive campus-based retention program. It should be noted that nothing here is completely prescriptive. Readers should remember that it is indeed a "framework" and that the following ideas and strategies are guidelines to begin the design and implementation process on your college campus. In the end, each institution must develop its own strategy to be successful, as no one-size-fits-all approach exists. What lies beyond are strategies from the research literature to help in planning and development. The retention framework is classified into five components based on an extensive review of current literature (Figure 22). Four of the five components—financial aid, recruitment and admissions, academic services, and student services—are generally major departments in most four-year institutions. The fifth component, curriculum and instruction, is receiving more attention and consideration at colleges and was added to this study because of the direct impact it has on student retention. The framework components are further broken down into categories based on areas of specialization and subsequently into specific objectives.

It is important that practitioners understand the relationship between the framework's components. Most notable is the ability of campus departments to work together toward common goals and focus on students' needs (Noel, Levitze, and Saluri, 1985; Smith, Lippitt, and Sprandel, 1985). From an organizational perspective, it is difficult to imagine how any of the components could work effectively without links to other areas. For instance, financial aid offices work closely with recruitment and admissions offices, while academic services must work in tandem with departmental efforts in curriculum and instruction. The framework attempts to develop additional links, such as those between student services and academic services, where the notion of Tinto's theory of academic and social integration (1975, 1993) is most

FIGURE 22
Five Components of the Student Retention Framework

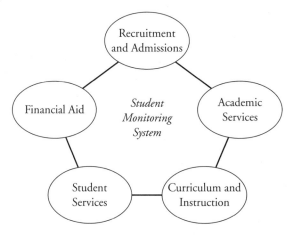

SOURCE: Swail, 1995.

relevant. The link of recruitment practices with precollege academic support programs is a good example of how a campus-wide support network can help students persist toward graduation. Thus, interrelation of the five components within the framework should be a major consideration for practitioners and developers.

As shown in Figure 22, the research-based framework is supported by a student monitoring system. The system, identified from literature and panel discussion as an important component of a campus-wide retention program, is a resource that supports the linkage of campus components or services. Such a system, when developed to capture data that reflect the true nature of student and faculty life, provides institutions with a snapshot of student experience in terms of academic and social development (Tinto, 1993). It is with this knowledge that campus offices and personnel can generate more appropriate methods of supporting students' needs. To make this system useful, institutions must ask the appropriate questions and be willing to enact systems to collect data that can answer those questions. It can be a huge amount of work, but it is undoubtedly the only way of answering the difficult but important questions that relate to student persistence.

Component One: Financial Aid

Financial aid is a critical part of the persistence puzzle. For students from low-income backgrounds, many of whom are students of color, finances are a make-it or break-it issue. A strong financial aid office is often the sign of a well-oiled campus, where latitude is given to students who have special financial needs.

Four categories were used to describe financial aid (see Figure 23). Grants and scholarships, student loans, financial counseling, and assistantships/work-study programs were all identified in the literature and supported by the panel to be important factors in student retention.

Although research has shown that grants are a much better predictor of students' persistence than loans (Astin, 1982; U.S. General Accounting Office, 1995), the finite limitations on the availability of grants and scholarships suggest that loans and work-study options must remain open avenues for students to gain access to the nation's postsecondary institutions. Princeton, Stanford, and a host of other Ivy League campuses have made news in recent years by making

FIGURE 23
Financial Aid Component

1 Financial Aid	
1.1 Financial Aid Counseling/ Training **1.1.1** Improve the flow and ease of information to students and families regarding college financing options. **1.1.2** Ensure that prospective students and families receive aid and other college information early. **1.1.3** Collaborate with financial management professionals to offer financial management seminars to students and families. **1.1.4** Provide financial aid counselors with cultural diversity/sensitivity training.	**1.3 Loans** **1.3.1** Educate students and family members about student loan obligations. **1.3.2** Streamline bureaucracy and forms to simplify loan application process. **1.3.3** Integrate mandatory career development with student borrowing. **1.3.4** Provide emergency loans to students in need.
1.2 Grants and Scholarships **1.2.1** Maximize availability of grant and scholarship aid compared with student loans. **1.2.2.** Create additional sources of grant and scholarship aid through the private sector. **1.2.3** Ensure that funds are available to provide emergency grants to students as required.	**1.4 Assistantships and Work-study** **1.4.1** Expand assistantships and work-study programs for undergraduates. **1.4.2.** Restrict assistantships and work-study to 15–25 hours per week for full-time undergraduates. **1.4.3** Partner with area businesses in close proximity to campus to forge assistantships and research opportunities for undergraduates. **1.4.4** Create opportunities with public and private businesses that lead to employment after graduation with "loan forgiveness" compensation plans.

large commitments to need-based aid,[4] but the reality outside of a handful of institutions in our entire postsecondary system suggests that colleges must develop increasingly creative and alternative ways to increase institutional aid for needy students, especially at moderately priced private institutions.

[4]In early 1998, Princeton University made public that it would spend an additional $6 million a year providing aid to low-income students. Within a month, both Yale and Stanford followed suit with similar promises. Although most financial aid experts applauded the news, the underlying comment from the majority was that these institutions "could afford it."

Although some ethnic groups historically are averse to financial debt (Thomas, 1986), loans are nonetheless a standard component of most financial aid packages. Institutions must consistently review their packaging procedures and ensure that students and families are educated about the loan process and that the loan represents a long-term investment against future returns. The delivery of accurate and easy-to-follow information regarding loan availability and regulations is an important factor for families.

A major barrier to access and persistence is the lack of information for parents and students regarding grants, loans, and scholarship opportunities. Colleges must be proactive in advising families of the price of college,[5] selection criteria, and availability of financial aid opportunities. The application process must also be designed such that it does not deter families from applying for financial aid (Astin, 1982; Collison, 1988). In the late 1990s, the U.S. Department of Education conducted focus groups and video profiles of parents and families completing the Free Application for Federal Student Aid (FAFSA) form, which must be completed by all students applying for federal aid in the United States. The department found that most families, from all income levels, had trouble completing the form. Although the Student Financial Aid office within the U.S. Department of Education has made strides in this area, the financial aid process is still a maze and deterrent for many families.

One other area for consideration is the availability of emergency loans and grants for students who occasionally require additional financial support midway through a semester as a result of unanticipated costs associated with books, health care, and travel. The availability of quick turnaround funds for students can help students focus on their studies and persist through the semester.

Assistantships and work-study programs can be an important part of a student's college education, especially for science majors. Astin (1975), for example, found that work-study programs could increase student persistence by 15 percent. These opportunities provide students with money, experience in the field, and, perhaps most important, networking capabilities for future

[5]Much of the discussion of the "cost" of college has been confusing to those in higher education, let alone parents and students. To this end, and in accordance with the recent report from the National Commission on the Cost of Higher Education (1998), the amount that students and parents pay as "price" and "cost" refers to the cost associated with supplying education.

employment and research possibilities. Recent research by NCES (Horn, 1998), however, supports Astin's finding a threshold exists where the amount of work per week distracts students from their studies and lowers the chances of a student's persisting.[6]

Financial counseling is the foundation for grants, loans, and work-study programs. Counseling allows campuses to reach out to families and students and offer a variety of avenues to finance college attendance. College financing is arguably one of the most important and costly endeavors a family may make, and financial aid staff must be cognizant of the burden these decisions place on families and provide excellent support for them during the decision-making process. Additionally, families need information early. Colleges can work with school systems to develop financial aid nights.[7]

The financial aid portion of the framework has three major objectives:

1. *Disseminate information.* To make informed decisions, appropriate information must get to students and families regarding student financial aid. The use of new technologies to deliver this information, such as computer networks and computer-interactive systems, can help families plan for college and learn more about the college environment and requirements. A number of college cost calculators are on the Web, and institutions can link into them. They are useful, however, only if the targeted constituencies use them. Institutions must devise efficient and coherent communication paths to interested families in a method that is both informative and supportive. Yet access to these new technologies, especially computers and the Internet, is heavily influenced by family income. Thus, traditional information or access to computer-aided information must also be made available.

2. *Increase availability of need-based aid.* Colleges should attempt to revise current lending practices to increase the availability of grants, scholarships, work-study programs, and loans to needy families. Much of the availability is based on federal authority, but institutions still make key

[6]Both Astin's and NCES's research found that students who worked about fifteen hours generally persisted more than other students. Those who worked more hours tended to have higher rates of departure.
[7]The National Association of Student Financial Aid Administrators (NASFAA) helps coordinate financial aid nights around the country. For more information, see http://www.nasfaa.org.

decisions on institutional and other aid. A case in point is the trend to move toward merit-based aid on campus. Colleges should consider the impact of those decisions and maximize aid to needy students. The revision of current national financial aid policies, although beyond the control of individual colleges, must be watched carefully by college administrators and national collegiate association representatives.

3. *Reconsider aid packaging.* Steady increases of tuition and fees require creative packaging, especially for students from low-income backgrounds but also for all students. The packaging of federal aid is legislatively controlled, and some private aid, such as the "last dollar" programs, has certain restrictions on how they are packaged with other aid components. Institutions have more flexibility with their institutional aid, however, and can use it in a variety of ways (for example, merit, supplementary need-based grants). Some research shows that front-loading student aid packages (that is, coordinating financial disbursement so that students receive more money during the freshman year and diminished amounts in subsequent years) results in a more efficient use of loan money (U.S. General Accounting Office, 1995) and can help students get over the hump of their college experience. Many financial aid practitioners are wary of that practice, however, and would rather use it in other ways.

Component Two: Recruitment and Admissions

The development of enrollment management programs in recent years has empowered the recruitment and admissions staff on many campuses. From an institutional perspective, how an institution "chooses" its prospective students and what financial aid it offers is the crux of institutional business. Institutions must be cognizant of the issue of institution-student fit, and at some point the business side must regress to allow for the personal side of the college connection. Ultimately, college is a service industry, and the student is the client.

The three categories under the classification of recruitment and admissions include student identification, admissions, and orientation (see Figure 24).

Tinto (1993) and other researchers (Astin, 1975; Cope and Hannah, 1975) discuss the importance of matching students' goals and expectations to a

FIGURE 24
Recruitment and Admissions Component

2 Recruitment and Admissions	
2.1 Student Identification **2.1.1** Collaborate with pre-college programs and high school counselors to identify prospective recruits. **2.1.2** Develop outreach programs that target the student demographics of interest to the institution. **2.1.3** Monitor the participation of students enrolled in pre-college programs. **2.1.4** Conduct on-campus orientation activities for counselors and teachers from local secondary school and pre-college. **2.1.5** Include work-study students and education majors on college recruitment teams to inform middle and high school students of the academic, social, and financial requirements for college participation. **2.1.6** Coordinate recruitment with alumni associations to identify prospective students.	**2.2 Admissions** **2.2.1** Identify students' academic and career goals and use to develop match with those of the institution. **2.2.2** Establish admissions criteria using a holistic approach for a more comprehensive assessment of students' commitment to college and compatibility with the institution. **2.2.3** Evaluate the use of college admissions tests scores in admissions profiles to ensure an appropriate mix of criteria in the admissions formula. **2.3 Orientation** **2.3.1** Provide opportunities for pre-college secondary school students to live on campus. **2.3.2** Provide early student orientation activities for students and families. **2.3.3** Involve all campus departments in the student orientation process. **2.3.4** Provide orientations at satellite locations for non-local students. **2.3.5** Ensure personal communications with students and families via telephone and visitations. **2.3.6** Institute freshmen orientations as credited course requirements.

college's mission. The role of the recruitment and admissions offices must be clarified, first, to identify students whose career and educational goals are closely matched to the institutional mission and, second, to admit only those students to college.

Focus areas under this category include the recruitment of students who have been involved in precollege preparatory programs, promotional visits to local secondary schools, the development of outreach programs in the institution's target area, and the use and promotion of alumni clubs to recruit students.

Although traditional admissions practice incorporates some level of student assessment to verify institutional fit, the process is not as sophisticated as it could be. Colleges should use a number of assessment and evaluation practices in the admissions office to determine the extent of student-institution congruence. Although the majority of four-year colleges widely use SATs and other norm-referenced tests for gatekeeping, they are by no means the only measures of students' ability or aptitude. Even the College Board strongly advises that the SAT should be used only in conjunction with other measures, such as GPA, class rank, and other noncognitive measures, including essays and interviews.[8] Additionally, colleges should consider that the admissions process is also an opportunity to accept the reciprocal responsibility of ensuring that the institution fits the student. The admissions process is primarily about service to students, not gatekeeping, even though gatekeeping is a definitive role in the admissions process.

Finally, the campus orientation aspect of this component is an important part of student integration on campus, both socially and academically. Orientation should look beyond the student and offer opportunities to families and significant others, as the college experience is truly an experience for the entire family and not just the person in attendance. The Lubin House experience at Syracuse University (Elam, 1989) remains an exemplary model of satellite orientation practice that other colleges should study carefully. Additionally, on-site orientation and extensive communications with families should become standard practice for any college.

The recruitment and admissions segment of the framework has five major objectives:

1. *Precollege programs.* To ensure the efficiency of campus offices related to student recruitment, coordinators should capitalize on student data and involvement in precollege programs offered by the institution. Students in these programs generally have already shown college aspirations and

[8]The College Board, in its annual press release about college-bound seniors each September (the release of SAT and advanced placement data), prominently makes note of the limitations of standardized test scores and the dangers of using them without other indicators. Further information on this issues may be found at http://www.collegeboard.org.

academic potential, and have been oriented to the college. Therefore, pre-college programs offer institutions an opportunity to recruit and assess student ability based on previous contact with students and schools.

2. *Alternative assessment methods.* Colleges can revise current selection criteria to include a variety of assessment techniques, including portfolios, interviews, and perhaps other nontraditional methods of pretesting. Although there is concern over the cultural bias of SAT testing (Kalechstein and others, 1981; Dreisbach and Keogh, 1982; Steele, 1999; Jencks and Phillips, 1998; Guinier, 2001), most empirical research finds SATs and the academic rigor and selection of high school courses to be the best predictors of student persistence and success (Sedlacek and Prieto, 1990; Adelman, 1999).

3. *School visitations.* The use of work-study students, graduate assistants, and other student personnel to make visits to local high schools (especially their alma maters) in the capacity of recruiter is a cost-effective way of reaching out to the community. This practice is appealing because of the close connection between college students and high school students as opposed to trying to bridge the gap with recruitment personnel. These interactions also help generate a peer relationship between the college and high school that may be an important part of a student's decision to attend college or a particular campus.

4. *On-campus living orientation.* Providing high school students enrolled in precollege programs with on-campus experiences, especially living opportunities, can have long-term positive impacts on their aspiration for post-secondary studies. This practice has practical applications for both students and colleges: it gives students opportunities to test the college environment and become more familiar and comfortable with the college, and it allows colleges a much better chance of recruiting students who have had extended visits to the campus.

5. *Freshman orientation.* Linking freshman orientation programs with course credit generally increases students' interest and attention and justifies their importance to students in relation to their academic pursuits. Some universities have designed one–, two–, or three–credit hour programs for first-semester students. Although the establishment of mandatory orientation

without credit is a standard practice on many campuses, students often resent this use of their time, particularly when orientations are poorly planned and offer students little in terms of increased knowledge regarding university services and regulations or useful skills.

Component Three: Academic Services

The academic services component is the most diversified and expansive component in the framework (see Figure 25). The focus of academic services in terms of student retention and persistence is on providing supplementary support to students in addition to practice with classroom lectures. This component is divided into six categories: academic advising, supplementary instruction, tutoring and mentoring, research opportunities, precollege programming, and bridging programs.

Effective academic advising is important to laying out an appropriate course map for students (Forrest, 1982; Beal and Noel, 1980). To be effective, it is important that students receive guidance that reflects their needs and incorporates the knowledge of campus programming and bureaucratic practices. Prospective advisers need to be trained accordingly to handle a variety of issues during advising sessions.

Many campuses have initiated computer-based advising systems. Although these systems are cost-effective, they do not allow for the development of relationships or the interaction between adviser and student, an important opportunity to talk with the student about his or her progress.

Beal and Noel (1980) also noted the importance of using faculty as student advisers. This practice has many potential benefits in addition to the academic guidance that may be offered, including role modeling and mentoring. Faculty members must be appropriately briefed and trained on the institution's various issues and policies, however. This practice is not often followed at institutions.

Supplementary instruction programs are prominent on many colleges and university campuses. The supplementary instruction program developed at the University of Missouri–Kansas City is perhaps the most widespread program in use. In addition to providing remedial activities and supplementary support, however, departments must also continue to develop better strategies that increase knowledge acquisition and improve the learning process for all students.

FIGURE 25
Academic Services Component

3 Academic Services	
3.1 Academic Advising **3.1.1** Provide ongoing professional development opportunities for counseling staff. **3.1.2** Provide appropriate academic advising and counseling to students throughout the college experience. **3.1.3** If faculty members act as academic advisors, ensure that they are properly trained and are cognizant of specific policies, course structures, and credit requirements within the institution.	**3.4 Research Opportunities** **3.4.1** Support the development of faculty-student research projects. **3.4.2** Integrate regular research activities into curricula. **3.4.3** Develop partnerships with industry for research opportunities. **3.4.4** Collaborate with business and industry on in-class presentations and experiments.
3.2 Supplementary Instruction **3.2.1** Encourage the development of peer study groups to foster learning. **3.2.2** Incorporate more practical application exercises with class assignments. **3.2.3** Integrate a variety of Instructional methods to support student learning. **3.2.4** Employ peer instructors for supplementary instruction, when possible. **3.2.5** Develop academic learning centers to provide supplementary support for students. **3.2.6** Provide non-classroom opportunities for student-faculty interaction.	**3.5 Pre-College Programs** **3.5.1** Develop pre-college programs at elementary and secondary education levels. **3.5.2** Offer pre-college programs on and off campus. **3.5.3** Monitor students' progress in pre-college programs. **3.6 Bridging Programs** **3.6.1** Provide summer academic and social support for students requiring additional support during the summer before matriculation. **3.6.2** Provide on-campus residency to students during bridge program participation. **3.6.3** Monitor all students' progress in bridging programs.
3.3 Tutoring/Mentoring **3.3.1** Provide regularly scheduled, easy access tutoring to students for all courses. **3.3.2** Use Teaching Assistants (TAs), Research Assistants (RAs), and exemplary undergraduates as tutors. **3.3.3** Encourage peer tutoring and group studying within class population. **3.3.4** Encourage faculty members to support the academic development of students outside of class time. **3.3.5** Create incentives for faculty participation in mentoring programs. **3.3.6** Recruit a diverse mentoring staff of students, faculty, and staff.	

Tutoring and mentoring practices form another support network for students. Colleges must make tutoring support available and affordable to students with such need. Faculty members should also make themselves available for academic assistance. Many researchers have substantiated this out-of-classroom contact between students and faculty members as an important factor in student persistence (Ugbah and Williams, 1989; Griffen, 1992), with ramifications for the student's personal, social, and intellectual development (Griffen, 1992).

Students in science-based disciplines (social and physical) can benefit greatly from research opportunities. The link between classroom theory and real-world practice has positive implications for a student's retention of knowledge while also making him or her more marketable after graduation. The development of local business partnerships and encouragement of on-campus research can create excellent opportunities for students.

Precollege programs provide an opportunity for the campus to work actively with elementary and secondary students (Swail and Perna, 2002). The federally funded TRIO programs have provided support to low-income and other students for more than thirty years. As well, partnerships through the federal GEARUP (Gaining Early Awareness and Readiness for Undergraduate Programs) initiative have heightened awareness and interest among many colleges. Other regional programs such as MESA (Mathematics, Engineering, and Science Achievement) and MSEN (Mathematics and Science Education Network) are examples of how precollege programs can help motivate students toward those areas. Colleges can benefit greatly from the establishment of these and other programs and the ensuing partnerships with K–12 schools and community organizations.

Bridging programs are an offshoot of precollege programs but are more specific. Colleges can effectively use a high school student's senior year or summer before matriculation to help further develop and orient the student's knowledge and ability to meet freshman program requirements. Study skills, time management, and course-related study are popular content offerings.

The academic services portion of the framework has five major objectives:

1. *Academic advising.* Colleges should implement a regular and standard practice of academic advising for students. Students' attitudes are also directly

related to persistence, and a proactive advising system of checks and balances would require scheduled meetings to catch problems before they occur. Such meetings should be face to face, not moderated by computer.

2. *Diverse instruction.* Supplementary instruction programs should use a combination of successful instructional techniques that support learning preferences of the entire student audience. Online and distance education has helped raise the bar for teaching and learning on campus, and faculty need to be more aware of the interaction of teaching styles and pedagogy with student learning styles (Whimbey and others, 1980; Hyman, 1988).

3. *Bridging programs.* Colleges should focus on developing academic bridge programs between senior year in high school and the freshman year in college. On-campus intervention programs afford students a number of potential benefits, including opportunities to become acclimated to the campus, work through some freshman problems before the fall semester begins, receive academic support in areas of weakness, and become accustomed to the pace associated with college-level academic learning.

4. *Precollege programs.* To help develop the pipeline of students interested in attending college, institutions should place considerable resources into the development of precollege programs wherever possible and practical. These programs, provided at levels as early as elementary school, help motivate students, get them thinking about the possibility of college, and provide important academic support and college knowledge to students and their families (Swail, 2000).

5. *Informal faculty-student contact.* Colleges should try to promote informal contact between faculty members and students to build trust, support, and motivation during the college experience. Out-of-class contact with a student can create a bond and a sense of self-worth that can positively affect a student's locus of control and impact future decisions regarding college. Extra assistance on projects, informal discussions on academic subjects, and special social gatherings can encourage this type of interaction.

Component Four: Curriculum and Instruction

The continued development of curricula and pedagogical practice is perhaps the most important and fundamental need that colleges must address in terms of student retention (see Figure 26). The need to revise current practices, especially in gatekeeper courses, stems from what Tobias (1990) acknowledges as the practice of designing courses that are "unapologetically competitive, selective and intimidating, [and] designed to winnow out all but the 'top tier'" (p. 9).

Of primary importance to academic offices should be the continuous process of curriculum review and revision. This process should in fact become a mainstream component of curriculum development. Especially in terms of science, engineering, and mathematics, academic content must reflect the

FIGURE 26
Curriculum and Instruction Component

4 Curriculum and Instruction

4.1 Curriculum Review and Revision

4.1.1 Design curricula with interdisciplinary and real-world emphasis to stimulate interest and profound understanding on behalf of students.

4.1.2 Develop a continuous review process of curricula utilizing faculty, student, and outside consultation.

4.1.3 Incorporate current and innovative technologies into the curriculum.

4.2 Instructional Strategies

4.2.1 Incorporate interactive, relevant, hands-on, exploratory instructional practices.

4.2.2 Establish learning communities.

4.2.3 Integrate Supplemental Instruction into the curriculum.

4.2.4 Provide students with short- and long-term research and application assignments.

4.2.5 Utilize educational technologies to complement instruction.

4.3 Assessment Strategies

4.3.1 Develop assessment instruments that require students to utilize diverse cognitive skills.

4.3.2 Perform regular student testing and assessment to monitor student progress (standard question/answer tests, lab assignments, out-of-class assignments, observation, portfolios, etc.)

4.3.3 Employ early intervention programs to identify and assist students experiencing academic difficulty in each semester.

4.3.4 Develop digital monitoring system for instant trend analyses of student's achievement as determined by assessment tools.

4.4 Faculty Development/Resources

4.4.1 Provide appropriate in-service development opportunities for teaching faculty.

4.4.2 Establish teaching faculty reward system.

4.4.3 Create a center for teaching excellence to support faculty development.

4.4.4 Identify and/or provide grant opportunities for classroom research.

current dynamics of industry practice to be worthwhile and effective. Therefore, to prepare students for employment in science, engineering, and mathematics in the near future, it follows that science, engineering, and mathematics curricula must relate not only to current industry trends and practices but also to anticipated practices and procedures (for example, cutting-edge technology and research). Colleges should attempt to gain access to new equipment and provide instruction that uses state-of-the-art instructional technologies to ensure that materials are presented in a fashion that is commensurate with students' learning preferences. The communication age has radically altered traditional learning and teaching styles, especially for students currently in elementary and secondary classrooms. Computers are second nature to new students matriculating to college or attending precollege programs. Within a few years, virtual reality, a technology embodied as the ultimate in applied scientific and medical training, may also be second nature to undergraduates. Thus, colleges must allocate resources to the development of new teaching strategies that incorporate the latest in educational and industrial technology. Without these considerations, students may find upon graduation that their knowledge is not aligned with the needs of society, when they should be on the cutting edge.

With the revision of curricular and instructional approaches comes the need for a revision of assessment practices on campus. If new curricular practices focus on a higher level of knowledge and understanding for learners, assessment practices must be able to document this higher learning. Thus, traditional methods of student evaluation are not appropriate to meet the needs of emerging teaching practice. The incorporation of instruments that measure students' comprehension rather than memorization and use a variety of assessment methods may offer a more accurate picture of student development and comprehension.

Faculty members' ability to deliver materials in an exciting, interesting, and motivating manner is also essential to the quality of education delivered by an institution. Research has shown that student achievement is higher when smaller classes and groups are used. The hands-on and group collaborative approach made popular by the Emerging Scholars Program at Berkeley (Fullilove and Treisman, 1990) has shown that students, with specific reference to African Americans, are more likely to increase their academic performance than students not involved in these programs. In effect, instructors must begin to employ practices more popularly related to K–12 education to reach students effectively.

If these areas are to become standard practice, faculty must receive appropriate training and support. Faculty development activities, with specific focus on teaching and assessment strategies, must become a basic foundation for instructional practice at colleges. The possible implementation or restructuring of faculty reward systems could provide incentives for teaching on campus.

The curriculum and instruction portion of the framework has four major objectives:

1. *Instructional practices.* Colleges should attempt to use various methods of delivering content to students, focusing on comprehension rather than rote memorization. The use of hands-on, exploratory, and peer learning groups are a few methods of motivating students to learn. A good balance is the use of a variety of instructional methods rather than one dominant method.

2. *Curricular review.* Colleges should develop an integrated process of curriculum review to ensure that all pieces of the curriculum are up to date and relevant to society's needs. At many universities, individual faculty members are left in isolation to decide what to include in a course syllabus, leaving much to be desired in terms of quality control. This issue is of great relevance, considering that most faculty have little or no background in learning theory or educational practice. Therefore, a systemic and cyclical review process that allows for faculty to review all curricula on a rotating basis helps control the content delivered in classes. It also serves to keep curricula current.

3. *Professional development.* Colleges need to provide extensive and ongoing professional development to faculty and staff to incorporate new teaching strategies and assessment techniques. Faculty cannot be expected to teach specific, if not more standard, courses without opportunities to share and learn from others with different experiences. If colleges and universities are serious about teaching as a focus of their mission, then it is incumbent upon them to provide support for their instructional staff.

4. *Assessment.* Campuses should design and implement new multifaceted assessment techniques that regard the integrity of human learning and understanding. Teaching and learning practices that require students to evaluate, synthesize, analyze, and create also require new methods of assessing students' progress (Ryan and Kuhs, 1993; Bird, 1990).

Component Five: Student Services

As Tinto (1993) and others have suggested, students' "social integration" with the institution is an important factor in their ability to persist. The role of the student services office has evolved to deal with many of the issues facing students on campus. The atmosphere and climate of the university, reflected by how the institution treats and supports students and by the positive nature of peer relations on campus, is important to the self-esteem and confidence a student generates. Neisler (1992) concluded that personal, emotional, and family problems, in addition to feelings of isolation and adjustment to college life, are strong barriers to retention for African American students. Therefore, the campus must focus on developing an atmosphere that is supportive, safe, and pluralistic. The outcomes of this study found that campus climate, accessibility to campus, campus housing, and career and personal counseling are areas that should be considered in terms of their effect on student retention (see Figure 27).

Campus climate is not some intangible, abstract concept that just happens. More accurately stated, campus climate is the development of the beliefs and practices of the administration, faculty, staff, and students belonging to that institution. Therefore, it can be created and, to some degree, controlled. To develop a positive campus climate supportive of learning and human development, campuses should promote diversity on campus and extol the virtues of shared culture (Justiz, 1994). This practice allows colleges and universities to better reflect the changes in society and promote pluralism. Ensuring safety for students and providing social opportunities for students to forge new friendships and build trust with their fellow classmates are examples. The existence of student groups and organizations can also support a positive climate by integrating students into the campus environment.

Accessibility to campus is also an important concept for institutions to consider. Administrators must consider the use of flexible scheduling to allow

FIGURE 27
Student Services Component

5 Student Services

5.1 Campus Climate

5.1.1 Build a supportive pluralist environment for students by embracing multiculturalism through campus leadership, faculty, staff, student enrollments, curricula, programming, and campus artifacts.

5.1.2 Provide a safe campus for all students, faculty, staff, and visitors.

5.1.3 Support campus student organizations that help develop a positive campus culture.

5.1.4 Work with academic services to provide non-classroom opportunities for student-faculty interaction.

5.1.5 Develop social activities that build community among all campus constituencies, such as intramural sports and academics, convocations, homecoming, entertainment, etc.

5.3 Housing

5.3.1 Ensure affordable housing and meal plans.

5.3.2 Encourage on campus residency for undergraduates.

5.3.3 Provide the appropriate number of housing slots to meet the needs of the student body.

5.3.4 If college experiences a campus housing shortage, ensure on campus housing for underclassmen.

5.3.5 Provide campus residents housed off site with additional services to support campus integration.

5.3.8 Incorporate special living-learning housing options to further academically integrate students.

5.4 Accessibility/Transportation

5.4.1 Ensure transportation link with local area transit system for increased access to campus.

5.4.2 Offer classes in a variety of time-slots to permit flexible scheduling by students, including weekends and Friday-Saturday course combinations.

5.4.3 Utilize distance-learning technologies and practices to broaden and support student participation and allow increased flexibility of courses schedules.

5.5 Counseling

5.5.1 Provide counseling, psychological, and other health services to students to enhance coping strategies.

5.5.2 Provide career counseling that connects academic and financial advising to ensure students are following the proper path to reach their goals.

5.5.3 Offer counseling services cultural and racially sensitive.

5.5.4 Offer a variety of counseling resources (such as legal services and family counseling) and techniques, including individual, group, peer, computer, and video sessions as necessary.

students with different schedules to be able to enroll in classes required for graduation. Classes on weekends and evenings and online courses are alternatives. An additional consideration is the access of public transportation systems to campus. Students who have difficulty reaching the campus are less likely to persist, although the use of distance learning technologies may help alleviate these problems.

On-campus housing that integrates students with the campus is an important element directly related to students' persistence (Pascarella, 1984; Chickering, 1974; Astin, 1977; Pantages and Creedon, 1978). Colleges must ensure, however, that housing is accessible and affordable for students and offer choices in types of housing. Poor housing options can be a major deterrent to persistence.

Studies of the effects of counseling for at-risk (Steinmiller and Steinmiller, 1991), African American (Trippi and Cheatham, 1989), and first-generation students (Richardson and Skinner, 1992) confirm that counseling services are important components of student retention programs. Colleges must deal with the added stress and burden that today's students bring with them to campus. Counseling services must provide support for students in terms of social needs and career counseling and be accessible to students.

The student services portion of the framework has five major objectives:

1. *Diversity and multiculturalism.* Colleges can build a pluralistic environment by promoting diversity and multiculturalism through special programming and activities. Studies by Astin (1993a) and Justiz (1994) found that campuses embracing diversity and multiculturalism attracted student populations that were very positive, capable of change, and academically skilled.

2. *Flexible scheduling.* Allowing the scheduling of classes in a variety of time slots allows a broader constituency of students to attend classes. Many universities have fixed schedules that allow little flexibility in course selection. Although inflexibility is mostly because of budgetary reasons, there are instances when it occurs because faculty are too inflexible to try different schedules. Adding Saturday courses or moving courses around the schedule may allow students to enroll in more of the classes they need

during a semester rather than wait for a rotation when they have no conflict. The targeted use of distance education can also provide flexibility in scheduling.

3. *Career counseling.* Colleges must ensure that students are sent on an academic track that will direct them toward their career destination. Occasionally, students are advised to take certain courses that in reality are poor choices and may extend their attendance. Career and academic counselors must be well versed in the requirements, schedules, and policies regarding graduation and have a keen knowledge of what business and industry are looking for. This aim can be accomplished only through qualified counselors' expansive knowledge of individual students.

4. *Faculty-student interaction.* Informal contact between faculty members and students is part of a rich atmosphere of sharing and caring at college campuses. Students feel much more relaxed and cared for when faculty are committed to their success. As stated, the social integration of students is paramount to their persistence, enjoyment, and achievement in college. The willingness and acceptance of staff to rub shoulders with students beyond the confines of the classroom can have long-lasting effects.

5. *Room and board.* Comfortable housing and affordable meals are important considerations for students. Campuses should look at numerous plans allowing students to choose the type of housing that best meets their financial ability and living requirements. This decision impacts mature students with families, economically disadvantaged students, and students living far from home.

Monitoring Students' Progress

At the center of the framework is the student monitoring system. It is an important aspect of retaining students and, from an organizational perspective, is a critical part of a continuous-improvement process. Simply put, without data, there is no normative relationship with an organization's past, let alone with its future. The use of a monitoring system allows several events to take place. First, it allows university personnel to follow a student's progress and anticipate an expected need on his or her behalf. For example, a student's downward spiral of grades in physics, if identified by a faculty member or other staff member, can issue a warning that the student requires tutorial assistance and support to get back on track. Unless someone or some department is privy to the appropriate information, however, this student, like countless others, is likely to fall through the cracks.

A student monitoring system is also necessary to assess the impacts of interventions and other retention strategies. Tinto (1993) suggests that the development of such a system must first be student centered. That is, it must collect information on every aspect of student development and focus on that progress. The collection of information provides the institution with a snapshot of students' progress; according to Tinto, it should detail a student's social and academic experiences "as understood by students" (p. 214).

Tinto's description (1993) of a retention assessment system emphasizes three main requirements for success: the system must be comprehensive, longitudinal, and recursive:

The process must be comprehensive. The system must incorporate both quantitative and qualitative methods of data collection to ensure that a representative portrait is developed of each student. Surveys and other instruments can collect important information on student progress but are susceptible to low response rates. The use of qualitative methods, in the form of focus groups, interviews, and other designs, helps fill information gaps and triangulate the information.

The process must be longitudinal. Because the process of student withdrawal from higher education is longitudinal in nature, student assessment must also be longitudinal. Therefore, collection and monitoring of student progress must involve more than the freshman experience and preferably begin before students are officially admitted to the college. The advantage of this practice is that school officials can become aware of potential needs before the student comes to the campus. Thus, the college can prepare in advance for each student's social and academic needs.

The process must be recursive. Recursive refers to the continuing process of data collection to develop university-wide trends among the student body. Only through an ongoing collection and analysis of student and organizational data can trends be developed; analysis of these trends provides the normative reflection to identify successes and remaining challenges on campus. This data analysis, by nature, is an important component of continuous improvement.

Implementation and Leadership

> It's impossible to really innovate unless you can deal with all aspects of
> a problem. If you can only deal with yolks or whites, it's pretty hard to
> make an omelet.
>
> [Gene Amdahl, cited in Levitze and Noel, 1985, p. 351].

AMDAHL'S PHILOSOPHY is key to any success that a retention program may have at any university. The look at the big picture is an important need, as much of the literature suggests. Martin (1985) suggests that too many schools have focused on admission exercises and recruitment programs instead of focusing resources on an institution-wide program to reduce attrition. To put things in the right perspective, Astin (1993b) states that educators must look at issues from a system perspective rather than an institutional perspective and view educational institutions in the same light as other public service providers such as hospitals and clinics. Higher education is now at a stage where it must begin to look at the big picture and anticipate the needs of society as a whole and match them with the needs of students.

Tinto (1993) developed three principles of an effective retention program. First is that any program must be committed to the students it serves. A program should be focused on the targeted population and not to other factors that may cause the direction of the program to go out of focus. Second, an effective retention program must be committed to the education of all students, not just to some. Thus, although it may incorporate special interventions for special populations, a retention program must address the needs of all students for the institution to meet its mission of providing quality education to all. Third, an effective retention program must be committed to the development of supportive social and educational communities on campus. Again, ensuring the social and academic integration of students is, according to Tinto, the most important issue to contend with in terms of student persistence.

Important Organizational Considerations in Developing an Institution-Wide Retention Program

The development of any program at any university requires a multifaceted process incorporating all individuals involved. In terms of an institution-wide project, the advice of Flannery and others (1973) must be remembered: the entire institution must take part. From an institutional point of view, many things must happen on campus to ensure that positive change can take place.

In an examination of effective institutional practices at four-year institutions, Clewell and Ficklen (1986) identified several characteristics of institutions employing effective practice: the presence of stated policy; a high level of institutional commitment; institutionalization of the program; comprehensive services, dedicated staff, and strong faculty support; an atmosphere that allows students to participate without feeling stigmatized; and collection of data to monitor students' progress. Institutional focus is the key ingredient of this set of characteristics. Stated policy, institutional commitment, comprehensive service, supportive atmosphere, and the ability to assess progress all point to the importance of a collective vision and ownership on the part of the entire campus, including administration, faculty, staff, and especially students. Leadership and faculty ownership are key variables in a successful equation, and messages sent down from the top are critical to support from underneath.

Tinto (1993) offers a very useful set of action principles for implementation of a retention program:

1. Institutions should provide resources for program development and incentives for program participation that reach out to faculty and staff alike.

2. Institutions should commit themselves to a long-term process of program development.
3. Institutions should place ownership for institutional change in the hands of those across the campus who have to implement that change.
4. Institutional actions should be coordinated in a collaborative fashion to insure a systematic, campus-wide approach to student retention.
5. Institutions should act to insure that faculty and staff possess the skills needed to assist and educate their students.
6. Institutions should front-load their efforts on behalf of student retention.
7. Institutions and programs should continually assess their actions with an eye toward improvement.

As other models have established, the importance of assessment, ownership, collaboration, institution-wide coverage, and commitment are essential to Tinto's principles. In addition, the development of appropriate skills by the faculty and staff and the principle of front-loading the program for freshman students are acknowledged. Institution-wide change and the coordination of effort across all departments and levels are essential to real change. As Kanter (1983) notes, however, any change at the institutional or individual level is a complex phenomenon. In describing the interdependent nature of campus change, Smith, Lippitt, and Sprandel (1985) discuss the organizational nature of the college institution. In their discussion, the authors describe a set of four interdependent parts of the higher education structure that must interact to support change. First is a vertical set of relations between system levels, such as trustees, administrators, and faculty members. Second is a set of horizontal relations between departments, administrators, student organizations, and others. The third part is the element of time: past, present, and future. Smith, Lippitt, and Sprandel claim that the tradition of the past, the practice of the present, and the goals and perspectives of the future all are important perspectives to consider. The relation of the system and the environment, including political, physical, and economic, provides the final interdependent component.

The pursuit of institutional change, according to Smith, Lippitt, and Sprandel (1985), depends on the ability of those leading the change to orchestrate all of these parts, a process that often takes too much of the project's energy. These different interdependent parts of the organization are barriers to change. In addition, they also become barriers to communications between colleagues and levels.

In fact, the energy required to push through a large-scale retention program can often derail the entire process. Although it is true that much effort must be spent on coordination and team building to ensure acceptance across campus, the leadership of the effort must carefully weigh how much energy goes into planning and operation as it does into the actual interventions that make up the program. Team members that are burned out by the time the actual intervention comes to fruition will tend to bow out of the project when it truly counts.

Regardless of the structure of institutional change, Smith, Lippitt, and Sprandel (1985) also acknowledge the process of change. In particular, four levels of readiness must be attained to produce the desired results and must involve each of the four parts already acknowledged. Level One is a stage of *latency.* As suggested, there is no action at this point, no leadership or sanction. Not until the institution has reached Level Two, *awareness,* is there much acknowledgment of the project. At this level, the need for systemwide action is realized, but rarely without the aid of an internal or external consultant or expert. Level Three is the *intent to act* stage. Leadership lends its support publicly at this point, sending out supportive and formal messages. Finally, Level Four, *energy,* is where the project is put into action.

Implementing Campus-Wide Programs

Developing and implementing a comprehensive student retention program requires a commitment from leaders, faculty, and staff. Through our discussion with some of these individuals and our review of related research, we were able to come up with a short list of essential factors in establishing such a program. According to our research, a comprehensive student retention program must:

Rely on proven research. Given the resources and effort that must go into a campus-wide retention program, the final plan must be based on solid, proven evidence of success. It is a long way to travel with no idea of the outcome. If such an effort fails, the task of putting the pieces back together would be daunting, to say the least. Spend time looking at what works, and borrow from the best.

Suit the particular needs of the campus. Not all campuses are equal. That said, no "boxed" retention program works the same on any two campuses. All efforts must be shaped to meet the specific needs of each campus.

Institutionalize and become a regular part of campus service. Any program at the beginning is usually a special project supported by outside funds. In the end, however, any successful effort must be institutionalized with respect to funding, policy, and practice. Outside funding does not last forever, and stated policy ensures that any interventions can become a mainstay in campus-based practices.

Involve all campus departments and all campus personnel. Everyone must be involved at some level. The most successful practices engage the entire campus, while the least successful strategies are very compartmentalized. We have seen "campus-wide" programs that individuals in certain parts of campus never knew about. Of course, they failed. But those institutions that had a broad outreach among faculty and staff, with clearly stated policy and practical objectives, tended to be successful.

Take into consideration the dynamics of the change process and provide extensive and appropriate retraining of staff. Change is difficult and uncomfortable. Do not underestimate the impact of change on one's ability to push through policy changes on campus. Team members must be brought along and be given all opportunities to learn about the interventions and develop appropriate skills as necessary.

Focus on students. Although this statement sounds like a given, many programs end up making the effort about themselves and not the clients. Everything should point to how it affects students and persistence on campus. This mind-set is a good one for all institutional practice that often gets lost in the "career" mind-set of board members, administrators, faculty members, and staff. Students are central to all operations on a campus.

Ensure that the program is fiscally responsible. Soft monies (grants, for example) provide a good foundation for start-up, but they are not a long-term solution to persistence at any institution. An important component of a strategic plan for retention is to build in a long-term fiscal plan to ensure that the program can operate without external support.

Support institutional research in the monitoring of programs and students. Data and analysis on all interventions, programs, and, ultimately, students are the saving grace of any campus change model. One must have the numbers to show whether movement has been made, either positive or negative.

Be patient. All change takes time, and change theory tells us that change usually takes a negative tack before the eventual positive change occurs. Understand that this trend is a normal mode and that some negative changes will happen before the positive yield will be seen. Therefore, leaders and other team members must be patient and understand that this long-term effort will have its rough spots.

Be sensitive to students' needs and target the most needy student populations. All students can benefit from a retention effort on campus, whether through improved tutoring programs or increased need-based aid. Any program should target the neediest students on campus, however, knowing that others will benefit from any changes made.

The development of a campus-wide retention program requires supportive leadership, the willingness to evoke change on campus, and careful planning. If any of these essential factors is missing, the chances for success are limited. Once institutions have ensured that the climate for change exists and that the support and guidance of campus leadership is present, several steps or stages must take place: preplanning, planning, implementation, and program monitoring. This strategic process can be developed in line with an institution's strategic planning schedule.

Stage One: Preplanning

The preplanning stage provides campus leadership with the information necessary to identify challenges and issues that the campus must face. During this initial stage, the institution must:

- Analyze the size and scope of retention issues on campus
- Identify students' needs

- Assess the status and effectiveness of current retention strategies and programs on campus
- Identify institutional resources that could be used or redirected
- Identify successful retention strategies at other campuses

This information-collecting stage can be done internally, but it sometimes carries more weight when handled through an outside consultant in partnership with the leadership team. With a solid foundation of evidence, the project team stands a much better chance of other institutional partners' buying into the project. As well, this information will allow the committee to make prudent decisions about what direction to follow in Stage Two.

Stage Two: Planning

The planning stage is the longest stage of the developmental process, as special care must be taken to involve the entire campus in the creation of the program. This is where buy-in occurs across campus. The planning stage must carefully assess the research conducted in Stage One, develop a redefined sense of purpose and goals, and develop an appropriate retention plan that meets those goals. The main activities of Stage Two include:

- Refinement or enhancement of the college mission statement and goals
- Development of organizational strategies
- Identification of key stakeholders on or off campus and their roles in the retention process
- Assessment, presentation, and discussion of preplanning data
- Development of the retention program's components and operation strategies
- Development of an implementation plan

Stage Three: Implementation

The implementation of the retention program should be according to the plan devised during Stage Two. It is critical for the administration to provide support, both political and financial, during the implementation stage for any unforeseen circumstances and difficulties encountered.

Stage Four: Program Monitoring

The monitoring of the retention program is an essential practice that must be entrenched in the design of the system. Without the careful planning of an assessment strategy, the true value and effect of the program components can never be measured. The monitoring system should provide ongoing data to all campus personnel involved in the operation of the retention effort. The main practices include:

- Collecting data and analyzing program components and student performance
- Disseminating data to stakeholders
- Ensuring that conclusions based on program monitoring are incorporated in program revisions

Strategic Timing

With regard to the framework introduced in the previous chapter, Figure 28 provides a look at the timing of particular strategies. This chart helps us understand the scope of involvement and outreach by the institution. As can be seen, some of these strategies begin in elementary school, while others last throughout the college experience.

The Importance of Leadership on Student Retention

Many campuses have launched recruitment and retention programs geared toward improving the success rates of low-income and other disadvantaged students. These programs often use several strategies, such as faculty and student mentoring, peer advising, and academic and social counseling to encourage at-risk students to remain enrolled (Sallie Mae, 1999).

Less discussed, however, is the role of the president and other campus leaders in developing, designing, and implementing successful retention efforts. Yet prior research has demonstrated that senior leadership on campus is often the key ingredient needed to implement these programs. For example, Redd and Scott (1997) used data from the *AASCU/Sallie Mae National Retention*

FIGURE 28
Timeline of Interventions Relative to the Framework for Student Retention

TIMELINE OF INTERVENTION	Elem	MS	HS	Summer	Fresh	Soph	Junior	Sr.+
School Year	5	8	12		13	14	15	16
FINANCIAL AID								
1.1 Grants & Scholarships								
1.2 Loans								
1.3 Assistantships & Work Studies								
1.4 Financial Counseling								
RECRUITMENT AND ADMISSIONS								
2.1 Student identification								
2.2 Admissions								
2.3 Orientation								
ACADEMIC SERVICES								
3.1 Academic Advising								
3.2 Supplementary Instruction								
3.3 Tutoring/Mentoring								
3.4 Research Opportunities								
3.5 Pre-College Programs								
3.6 Bridging Programs								
CURRICULUM AND INSTRUCTION								
4.1 Curriculum Review & Revision					*ONGOING*			
4.2 Instructional Strategies					*ONGOING*			
4.3 Assessment Strategies					*ONGOING*			
SOCIAL SERVICES								
5.1 Campus Climate								
5.2 Accessibility/Transportation								
5.3 Housing								
5.4 Counseling								
STUDENT MONITORING								

Project to illustrate the effects of senior leadership on retention. On successful campus efforts, senior leadership plays two important roles. First, the president and his or her key cabinet officers regularly monitor their institution's progress toward clearly stated campus retention goals. Redd and Scott (1997) noted, "Nearly 90 percent of the high-rate colleges said that *'senior administrators regularly monitor information about progress in increasing retention and graduation rates of students'* was descriptive or very descriptive of their institutions, compared [with] 69.3 percent of the low-rate colleges" (pp. 19, 21).

Second, the campus chief executive officer is usually the one person at the institution who can bring all the interested parties—students, parents, other campus administrators, faculty, and staff—together toward the goals of retention. Sallie Mae, in its *Supporting the Historically Black College and University Mission: The Sallie Mae–HBCU Default Management Project* (1999), noted that the president must coordinate "strategies [that] can be developed to help increase student success. . . . The president must remain fully informed of the [campus's] activities and help each of these units contribute to the goal of raising student achievement. Only leadership from the president or chancellor can bring [campus] units together" for the purposes of raising retention rates (Sallie Mae, 1999, p. 10).

Presidents can play other roles as well in their institutions' efforts to improve retention. According to Earl S. Richardson, president of Morgan State University, an HBCU in Baltimore, the president should emphasize four areas on his or her campus to improve retention (E. S. Richardson, personal communication, December 2001):

- Increase need-based financial aid for low-income, at-risk students
- Require attention in classroom advising
- Use the campus's social and cultural activities to keep students focused
- Encourage academic advising outside the classroom

According to Richardson, however, presidents "need to deal with all four areas together. . . . Campuses must become a community for students" for retention efforts to succeed (E. S. Richardson, personal communication, December 2001). In many instances, the president is the one person on campus who can integrate all four areas and strategies to work cohesively and simultaneously for students (E. S. Richardson, personal communication, December 2001).

James Shanley, president of Fort Peck Community College, a tribal college in Poplar, Montana, adds that chief executives also "need to engage students and families. Students are driven by family issues. However, student services are often designed for working with students but not for working with families" (J. Shanley, personal communication, December 2001). Older, nontraditional students are particularly affected by "day care and other family issues that hinder retention" (J. Sain, personal communication, 2001). Senior administrators are best able to use their influence on campus to deal with these issues effectively.

Chief administrators' attitudes about retention can also influence its importance on campus. For example, one institution reported that its senior administrators use retention goals as part of the staff evaluation system. All faculty and other staff are evaluated on what efforts they have made to improve the recruitment and retention of minority students (P. Hladio, personal communication, 2001).

Lack of Presidential Engagement in Retention Issues

Despite the possible influence of presidents on retention, most presidents do not appear to be engaged in these issues. One former college president says that "few presidents understand retention, and fewer still have the courage to make the systematic changes necessary to improve retention" (R. C. Dickerson, personal communication, November 11, 2001). Another campus official adds that institutional leaders sometimes give only lip service to retention (J. Taylor, personal communication, 2001), partly because of the other pressures presidents face such as fundraising and faculty issues. For this reason, "[most] retention efforts usually emanate from other sources on campus—student affairs, academic affairs, or [the] student service office, where they understand and value . . . retention" (R. C. Dickerson, personal communication, November 11, 2001).

The financial aid office is another area that can fill the void on retention that presidents may leave (P. Hladio, personal communication, 2001). Often, "aid administrators need to be the ones to make contacts with students to go the extra mile" in achieving their degree goals (P. Hladio, personal communication, 2001). Aid administrators at some institutions have set up programs on their own volition to attract and retain students of color such as early awareness programs, campus visits, freshmen class seminars, and academic advising (P. Hladio, personal communication, 2001). Aid administrators and other campus officials have tried to make a "more proactive effort on retaining students" (T. Ross, personal communication, 2001).

Policy Questions

Although financial aid, alumni relations, and other administrators and departments on campus play an important role in retention, the major thrust for improving success for students—particularly students of color—must come from the president. The chief executive is the one person who can bring together other senior staff, faculty, and financial aid for the common purpose of improving retention. Unfortunately, presidents also have many other burdens to carry, particularly fundraising, relations with faculty, and other pressing needs of students and alumni (R. C. Dickerson, personal communication, 2001). For this reason, retention for minority students on many campuses may get little attention or few resources from the president's office. This situation may lead to several important questions for campus officials and policymakers interested in increasing the success of students of color on college campuses:

What incentives can be developed that will encourage campus leaders to become more directly involved with retention efforts? Should states begin to tie increases in allocations to public colleges and university systems with increases in retention rates? Or should trustees on individual campuses base increases in presidents' salaries and other benefits on the share of students who complete a degree successfully?

What models of successful campus leadership exist, and can these models be replicated? Can successful leadership strategies that are developed for white students also be used for students of color at HBCUs and other minority-serving institutions?

If senior administrators cannot or will not become more involved with retention issues, can other groups outside the campus community (for example, state policymakers, community service organizations, potential outside donors) increase their involvement?

These and other questions may help determine the extent to which college presidents and other senior campus leaders are willing and able to use their positions, expertise, and resources to increase retention. Although the future changes presidents may make seem cloudy at best, it *is* clear that, at a number of higher education institutions, presidents have not done enough to increase the number of underrepresented students on their campuses who leave school with degrees.

Final Thoughts

This report contains an enormous amount of information: background information and data analysis related to the retention of minority students, theoretical underpinnings of student retention and persistence, the illustration of concrete resources and activities for consideration and implementation of retention programs on college campuses. We close with some final perspectives related to student retention:

Institutional leadership. The ultimate success of a campus-wide retention effort depends on a number of leadership issues. First, retention programs must have unequivocal support from the office of the president or provost, involve the entire campus in shaping program operations, and keep ideology focused on the student. Increasing student retention rates is a complex issue requiring the involvement of the entire campus. Although departments and offices may conduct their own programs, it is not until the entire campus directs a unified effort at reducing attrition that large-scale changes can be seen. The development of a cross-university retention task force sends a message of urgency as well as a sign of support from the administration. This task force can help plan across departmental differences inherent in most university systems.

Funding priorities. Retention costs money, but the savings are easily recouped. If increased student persistence is the goal, appropriate funding must be made available in the general budget. Funding sends an important leadership message to all faculty and helps crystallize campus priorities.

Faculty reward systems. If faculty members are to turn more of their attention to student needs and teaching as a whole, the institution must incorporate these actions into the tenure structure. Current reward structures at most institutions deter faculty members from focusing on teaching. Tenure and promotion decisions are by and large based on a history of research and scholarship, which includes a candidate's record of academic publishing and success in obtaining sponsored-research funds.

Student-teacher interaction. Faculty support is not just a tenure issue. Classroom instruction requires time to develop the student-teacher interactions that can make a difference. Most faculty believe they are overburdened with advisees, faculty and dissertation committees, and bureaucratic affairs. To make real differences in these interactions, such burdens must be reduced.

Flexible planning. Student retention programs must be designed to match the characteristics and conditions at each campus. Programs that work well on one campus do not necessarily work well on another campus. The students, faculty, and institutional mission bring different aspects to the campus that makes it special, and these characteristics must be considered in the planning cycle.

Institutional research. Feedback is perhaps the most important aspect of program development, implementation, and sustainability. The campus institutional research office is potentially the greatest resource for campus leadership and faculty. With appropriate fiscal and material support, institutional research offices can provide responsive feedback regarding the impact of major initiatives or programs, down to students. Empirical information should be the foundation of any retention effort, and careful planning is necessary to ensure that appropriate indicators are selected and high-quality data collected. Additionally, systems must be put in place to ensure that this information is disseminated systematically to inform key stakeholders about progress toward goals.

Academic preparation and admissions. Recent affirmative action litigation has forced campuses to rethink their admissions practices. One brief year after Proposition 209, California institutions showed dramatic decreases in the admission rates of black and Latino students. One answer to this problem for colleges is to further encourage and develop the academic preparation of minority students. The divisions between preK–12 and postsecondary education are becoming more blurred all the time. Colleges and universities are coming to understand that they need to play a stronger role during the precollege years. Short of radical educational reform, institutions interested in admitting students of greater academic capacity must wade into the pool themselves. Precollege outreach programs have enjoyed great success in increasing the academic ability and motivation of young students at the elementary, middle, and high school levels.

College affordability. College pricing is a major factor in whether or not students go to college as well as where they go. Since 1980, tuition and fees at four-year public and private institutions have risen about 90 percent after adjusting for inflation and student aid has increased around 40 percent, while median family income[9] has increased only 9 percent (College Board, 2001b). Thus, for many low-income students, many of whom are non-Asian minorities, the affordability of postsecondary education has become a crisis. Colleges and state systems must continue to address price as a major disincentive for needy students.

Technology. Recent developments in Web-based technologies have begun to impact how colleges and universities can deliver instruction and how students and professors can communicate. The birth of the virtual university and proliferation of distance education courseware is forcing institutions to rethink how they do business. But the ability to benefit from technology is a product of technological access. Although technology has the potential to remove barriers of time and distance, it simultaneously may widen gaps in access between low- and high-income students—between the technological haves and have-nots. Technology is clearly a double-edged sword. It is difficult to imagine the collegiate experience without computer assistance in this day and age. Colleges and universities must take special care to ensure that students from all backgrounds enjoy access to and are comfortable with technology.

[9]For families with parents aged 45–54, the approximate age of families with college-age dependents.

Appendix A: Promising College Student Retention Programs

American River College

Beacon Program: Peer Assistant Learning (PAL) Program Goal: Help students master course materials and skills to improve academic success and retention.

Program Description: Trained learning assistants (students who successfully completed the class) work with groups of currently enrolled students for two hours each week outside the classroom. Collaborative activities that encourage participants to interact are the focus of group work.

Key Components: Faculty identify students who have people skills and who did well (grade A or B) or are doing well in a course, and ask students to participate. They must be willing to go through a one-semester group tutoring training program (one unit), meet with their learning group for two hours per week outside the classroom, and meet with the instructor one hour each week. They are paid $6.00 per hour for some of their training time and for all the hours of meeting time.

Evidence of Effectiveness: Data gathered over the last seven semesters show success rates (achieving an A, B, or C) average 85 percent, while that of non-participants in the same class is 57 percent. Fewer Beacon students drop classes (7 percent) when compared with their non-Beacon counterparts (27 percent). The program received exemplary program awards sponsored by the California Community Colleges Board of Governors (American River College, 2001).

Contact: Kathie Read or Marsha Reske, Beacon Program, American River College, 4700 College Oak Drive, Sacramento, CA 95841, Telephone: 916-484-8693

Saint Xavier University

Student Success Program Program Goal: Provide academic and personal support services for academically, economically, and physically challenged students until the participating students complete a baccalaureate degree.

Program Description: The Student Success Program (SSP) is one of eight hundred student support service programs on college campuses across the nation that receive Title IV TRIO grant funds. Counselors, advisers, and academic instructors work as a team to promote academic success. Students receive class advising, counseling (academic, career, and personal), freshman orientation, advocacy, peer mentoring cultural programming, and service-learning.

Key Components: The program consists of four full-time professional staff—a director, an academic adviser, a personal counselor, and a mathematics specialist—and twenty to thirty employed peer tutors or mentors. Although program staff invite all incoming students to apply to the program, they select applicants based on socioeconomic and academic need as well as their level of goal commitment. Peer mentors meet with student participants weekly and are responsible for their academic and social integration into the campus by modeling appropriate student behaviors and providing referrals to program services. The mathematics specialist teaches semester-long math workshops that include technology use, problem solving, and critical thinking. The staff monitor students' academic performance continuously and provide special interventions for students experiencing academic difficulties.

Evidence of Effectiveness: Although SSP and non-SSP 1997 graduating cohorts had comparable ACT composite scores, high school grade point averages, and college semester course loads, data showed the SSP cohort had a higher total persistence rate after seven semesters than the total persistence rate of the non-SSP cohort (58.9 percent versus 53.7 percent). In addition, the program appears to have a greater impact on the persistence rates of minority students who participate in the program than the rates of those who do not (Murphy and Fath, 1996).

Contact: Iraetta Lacey, director, Saint Xavier University, 3700 West 103rd Street, Room L111, Chicago, IL 60655, Telephone: 773-298-3330, E-mail: lacey@sxu.edu

The University of Texas at San Antonio

The Risk-Point Intervention Program Program Goal: Provide interventional academic support to first-year, first-time freshmen at a series of specified points when academic risk becomes observable.

Program Description: Program consists of five interventions to address risks that occur during the freshman year.

Key Components: The Risk Point 1 intervention consists of an academic development program (ADP), a five-week summer bridge program for freshmen admitted on a provisional basis, and Risk Point 2 college success seminar (EDP 1702). New freshmen admitted on probation are required to enroll. The midterm checkpoint conference is a midsemester intervention program developed for first-time freshmen who receive D's or F's on their midterm progress reports. Academic counselors and freshmen meet to carefully review the student's performance to date and area(s) where academic difficulty has been exhibited. Phoenix is a probation recovery workshop for small groups of first-time freshmen who entered in good standing but have earned a GPA below 2.0 (placing them on academic probation at the end of their initial semester) work out a highly structured recovery plan. This plan involves strategic advising recommendations, reduction of outside workload, future course sequencing, and improved use of available institutional resource programs. Reentry provides academic assistance and guidance for specially readmitted, academically dismissed students. This program provides a careful evaluation of each student's academic skill, attitudes, awareness, and previously exhibited academic behaviors. Reentry students are required to repeat failed courses, reduce work and course loads, and participate in a structured program of support.

Evidence of Effectiveness: ADP participants have a one-year retention rate that is twice that of nonparticipants. During its first semester of implementation, probation students enrolled in the seminar were dismissed at a 15 percent lower rate than were nonparticipants. Checkpoint conference participants go on probation at a 7 to 15 percent lower rate than do nonparticipants. Phoenix participants are dismissed at a rate that is 8 to 12 percent lower than other first probation students who do not attend.

Contact: Tomás Rivera Center for Student Success, University of Texas at San Antonio, 6900 North Loop 1604 West, San Antonio, TX 78249, Telephone: 210-458-5170, Fax: 210-458-4695

William Paterson College

Sponsored Student Program Program Goal: Improve retention rates of special-admit students, who are 10 percent of the student population.

Program Description: The program allows the college to admit and support a limited number of students whose academic credentials fall below the institution's standard admissions criteria. Although special-admit students do not possess the college's academic requirements, they do indicate that they can be successful in college. The program combines developmental advising, mandatory personal academic counseling, and referrals to tutoring and other academic support services.

Key Components: Program participants take college placement exams and receive special academic advising for selection of courses and tutorial assistance. In addition, students with more demanding schedules or responsibilities are limited to taking thirteen credit hours per semester. Once a student achieves an acceptable grade point average and completes all prerequisites, he/she can declare a major.

Evidence of Effectiveness: Since 1990, sponsored student program participants consistently have had higher retention rates after one year than regular-admit students, educational opportunity program students, and nontraditional student cohorts (Spatz, 1995).

Contact: Mary Ann Spatz, Academic Support Center, Hunziker Wing 218 William Paterson University, 300 Pompton Road, Wayne, NJ 07470, Telephone: 973-720-3324, E-mail: spatzm@wpunj.edu

Wayne State University

Wayne State University Retention Program (Excel) Program Goal: Increase rate of student reenrollment; facilitate academic success and undergraduate achievement; enhance graduation rates.

Program Description: The program served as a pilot for offering high-level advising and academic support services to regular-admit undergraduates who exhibit academic and demographic risk for college persistence.

Key Components: The program uses qualified staff to provide mandatory orientation sessions, developmental student advising, an early academic warning system, personal tutoring, weekly supplemental instruction, and, if recommended, enrollment in developmental reading, learning theory, or vocabulary building courses.

Evidence of Effectiveness: Students participating in Wayne Excel had lower stopout and dropout rates than did students with similar risk factors who did not participate. Excel students entered probation status at a lower rate than did comparison groups. The institution expanded undergraduate retention services to all students, because the pilot program was effective in retaining students (Wilhelm and Wallace, 1997).

Contact: Academic Success Center, Wayne State University, 2100 David Adamany Undergraduate Library, Detroit, MI 48202, Telephone 313-577-3165

Southeast Missouri State University

First-year Learning Team (FLighT) Program Program Goal: Offer a top-quality curriculum, enhance student success and retention, and optimize and stabilize enrollment.

Program Description: The program provides freshmen with one of six holistic learning and living community experiences that assist them in the academic and social transition to college life.

Key Components: A FLighT consists of twenty-five students who are enrolled in two courses centered around a particular theme or area of interest. Each FLighT has a peer mentor, a veteran student who works closely with the group.

Evidence of Effectiveness: The fall 1998 to spring 1999 retention rate for FLighT students was 89 percent. The institution is tracking retention rates for subsequent semesters (Myers and Birk, 1998).

Contact: New Student Programs, 308 Academic Hall, Mail Stop 3850, One University Plaza, Cape Girardeau, MO 63701, Telephone: 573-651-5166, Fax: 573-651-5168

Fayetteville State University

Freshman Year Initiative (FYI) Program Goal: To ensure students' successful transition to college by identifying those students who experience difficulties in their first year of college and providing them with remedial help.

Program Description: The comprehensive retention program provides a gamut of academic and personal support services.

Key Components: Newly admitted students receive information about FYI and encouragement for participation. Students complete profiles and register in a block of courses based on intended major. Some students must complete math laboratory and/or reading/writing center assignments. All students enroll in Freshman Seminar I and II, where a peer academic leader is available.

Evidence of Effectiveness: Assessment data of freshman cohorts receiving FYI services reflect improved retention rates and increased student satisfaction (Young, 1999).

Contact: Olivia D. Chavis, vice-chancellor for student affairs, Fayetteville State University, W. R. Collins Building, Room 224, 1200 Murchison Road, Fayetteville, NC 28301-4298, Telephone: 910-672-1201, Fax: 910-672-1456

Loyola University New Orleans

Campus-wide Student Success Initiative Program Goal: Develop and provide services to assist students and faculty with improving student writing skills to successfully complete coursework.

Program Description: Help faculty design writing assignments for their courses and help students develop the skills they need to make the most of their learning experiences.

Key Components: Writing Across the Curriculum (WAC) services include full-class tutoring services through the advise/revise program; workshops in writing, grammar, documentation, and research; writing resource library and faculty resource bank, and *WAC Works,* a student newsletter on writing-related issues.

Evidence of Effectiveness: None found.

Contact: Melanie McKay, director, Bobet 100, Campus Box 40, Loyola University New Orleans, 6363 St. Charles Avenue, New Orleans, LA 70118, Telephone: 504-865-2297, E-mail: wac@loyno.edu

Northern Illinois University

Office of Retention Programs Program Goal: Develop, coordinate, and implement programs and services to assist students with successful degree completion.

Program Description: The Office of Retention Programs fosters interaction among students, faculty, and staff to provide the academic and personal support necessary for students to complete degree requirements.

Key Components: This holistic university retention model includes academic support services, orientation programs and courses, and innovative learning opportunities and initiative by each college. Programs include educational services and programs, learning assistance and study skills lab, academic information and referral services, tutoring, new student welcome days, passport to success, undergraduate research apprenticeship program, academic residential programs, university honors program, and smart classrooms.

Evidence of Effectiveness: None found.

Contact: Don Bramlett, director, Office of Retention Programs, Northern Illinois University, Adams Hall, Lucinda Avenue, Telephone: 815-753-7822, Fax: 815-753-7830, URL: http://www.niu.edu/retention/

Long Beach City College

Student and Teacher Achieving Results (STAR) Program Goal: Increase success and retention rates of underrepresented students.

Program Description: STAR creates a learning community by developing communities of student cohorts and linking courses through a theme.

Key Components: STAR students participate in linked courses that develop communication skills, use interdisciplinary curricula and cooperative learning, facilitate student involvement with faculty, build self-esteem, and provide academic and social support.

Evidence of Effectiveness: Data indicate that STAR significantly improved participants' reading and writing skills, advanced increased numbers of underrepresented students to higher-level courses, reduced the number of underrepresented students on probation, and increased retention and completion rates for underrepresented students (Couch and Holmes, 1997).

Contact: Long Beach City College, 4901 E. Carson Street Long Beach, CA, 90806–5797. URL: http://t3.lbcc.cc.ca.us/star.html

Glendale Community College

Student Pal Program Program Goal: Target and identify characteristics of at-risk students to improve the retention and success of minority students.

Program Description: The system provides data on specific student groups to fulfill the needs of administrators, faculty, student support staff, and researchers.

Key Components: Readily available data allow for analyses of student stopout and dropout patterns, GPAs, and other data relevant to students' success and retention.

Evidence of Effectiveness: The system has enhanced the multicultural affairs program's ability to fulfill goals and initiatives. The program also helped the institution initiate an early warning retention system for at-risk students (Mendoza and Corzo, 1996).

Contact: Jose Mendoza, director, Multicultural Affairs Program, 6000 West Olive Avenue, Glendale, AZ 85302, Telephone: 623-845-3565

Bronx Community College

Freshman Year Initiative Program (FYIP) Program Goal: Promote student growth, academic achievement, and retention.

Program Description: The program is a comprehensive academic and counseling program for a selective group of first-semester students who require at least three remedial courses.

Key Components: This program consists of five major components offering intensive counseling: (1) the Freshman Outreach, Caring, Understanding, and Support (FOCUS) Center, a holistic counseling center that offers personal and confidential counseling services; (2) psychoeducational testing; (3) peer counseling; (4) rapid contact counseling for early intervention; and (5) revised orientation and career development courses for personal development and improved coping skills.

Evidence of Effectiveness: Data show 76.5 percent of FYIP students continued enrollment from fall 1993 to fall 1997, compared with 59.3 percent of nonparticipants.

Contact: Jason Finkelsein, Freshman Year Initiative Program, University Avenue at West 181 Street, Bronx, NY 10453, Telephone: 718-289-5138

University of South Carolina

University 101 Program Goal: Support first-year students' college success.

Program Description: The three–credit hour elective course consists of a maximum of twenty-five students who interact with instructors to develop note-taking, study, time-management, and coping skills. The Freshman Year Experience and the First-Year Experience are trademarks of the University of South Carolina. A license to use these terms in educational programs may be granted upon written request.

Key Components: Students are able to develop these skills through frequent writing assignments, midterm and final exams, a library research project, and the use of course textbooks.

Evidence of Effectiveness: Studies show that students who take University 101 tend to graduate and exceed their predicted GPAs at higher levels than students who do not take the course (National Resource Center for the First-Year Experience and Students in Transition, 1999; Stanley and Witten, 1990).

Contact: Dan Berman, director of instruction and faculty development, National Resource Center for the First-Year Experience and Students in Transition, 1629 Pendleton Street, University of South Carolina, Columbia, SC 29208, Telephone: 803-777-6029, Fax: 803-777-4699, URL: http://www.sc.edu/fye/101/u101.htm

University 401 Program Goal: Support student's transition out of the university and document learning outcomes of institution's core curriculum.

Program Description: The program integrates seniors' major programs of study and general education into a larger context, provides opportunities for advance research, and transitions seniors for graduate school and employment.

Key Components: The program requires reading, writing, computing, and research that include a class team project; a portfolio; a liberal arts interdisciplinary exercise or project; and self-assessment and career planning exercises.

Evidence of Effectiveness: None found.

Contact: URL: http://www.sc.edu/fye/401/401infopiece/content.htm

Indiana Wesleyan University

Program Goal: Improve student retention.

Program Description: The program adopted a team approach to assess and counsel students regarding academic performance and financial aid.

Key Components: The institution developed regular academic and financial checkpoints to monitor academic performance of student borrowers and identify warning signs. The team adjusts financial aid and course-taking strategies to facilitate student program completion.

Evidence of effectiveness: None found.

Contact: Lois Kelly, assistant vice president for financial aid, Indiana Wesleyan University, 4201 South Washington Street, Marion, Indiana 46953-4974, Telephone: 765-677-2116, E-mail: lkelly@indwes.edu

West Virginia University

Structured Academic Year (STAY) Program

Program Goal: Retain students on academic probation by providing support to succeed academically.

Program Description: The two-semester program requires students to live in a structured campus environment with two resident assistants so they can improve their study skills and raise their grades.

Key Components: Students adhere to rigorous program requirements such as curfews, structured study periods and tutoring, group meetings, biweekly meetings with assigned academic advisers, career exploration, and regular interactions with mentors. Parental involvement is a critical component of the program.

Evidence of Effectiveness: Program participants raise their cumulative GPAs an average half a letter grade after one semester and one whole letter grade after two semesters. Most students complete the programs successfully and remain at West Virginia University.

Contact: Maria Watson, senior program coordinator, Academic Services Center, P.O. Box 6212, West Virginia University, Morgantown, WV 26506-6212, Telephone: 304-293-5805, ext. 320

EXCEL Program Goal: Improve students' academic success and retention.

Program Description: The structured voluntary program supports freshmen with high school GPA of 2.0 to 2.6.

Key Components: Students attend a special orientation class, receive assistance with academic skills, and participate in Orientation 101, facilitated by the assigned academic adviser.

Evidence of Effectiveness: EXCEL students achieved a quarter point higher GPA than WVU freshmen with comparable high school GPAs who were not in the program (2.15 versus 1.88); retention was 96 percent for EXCEL students as opposed to 84.5 percent for the control group.

Contact: Maria Watson, senior program coordinator, Academic Services Center, P.O. Box 6212, West Virginia University, Morgantown, WV 26506-6212, Telephone: 304-293-5805, ext. 320

University of Colorado at Boulder

Building Community Model Program goal: Recruit, retain, and graduate underrepresented students.

Program Description: The integrated model consists of five primary components for student development and retention.

Key Components: The integrated program consists of the Summer Bridge Program, SEED Freshman Leadership Course, Academic Clustering, Academic Excellence Workshops, and Financial Aid Tutoring; counseling and mentoring are integral parts of the program.

Evidence of Effectiveness: Approximately 85 percent of the forty new Multicultural Engineering Program (MEP) students registered for fall 1996 returned for the following academic year.

Contact: URL: http://www.colorado.edu/UCB/AcademicAffairs/ArtsSciences/masp/

Bowie State University

Model Institutions for Excellence (MIE) Program Goal: Serve as a model for the successful recruitment, education, and production of quality trained science, engineering, and mathematics baccalaureates.

Program Description: The MIE program provides support for institutional development and student support activities that contribute to the successful recruitment and retention of science, engineering, and mathematics undergraduates throughout the pipeline. Conceived by Walter Massey, then-director of the National Science Foundation, MIE is an eleven-year collaborative program. The National Aeronautics and Space Administration sponsors the Bowie MIE program in collaboration with the National Science Foundation. Other institutions with MIE programs are Oglala Lakota College (South Dakota), Spelman College (Georgia), Universidad Metropolitana (Puerto Rico), University of Texas at El Paso, and Xavier University of Louisiana.

Key Components: Students receive financial aid and participate in academic enrichment activities, early research, mentoring, counseling, and orientation to science, engineering, and mathematics graduate school.

Evidence of Effectiveness: Statistical data for fall 1995 to fall 2000 showed an increase in the institution's science, engineering, and mathematics undergraduate enrollment by 115 percent, from 340 to 733. Data also indicated an increase in retention of science, engineering, and mathematics first-year students by 28 points, from 52 percent to 80 percent, and by 39 points for second-year students, from 26 percent to 62 percent. Science, engineering, and mathematics student graduation rates increased 62 percent, from 56 to 91.

Contact: Thurgood Marshall Library, Suite 272, 14000 Jericho Park Road, Bowie, MD 20715, Telephone: 301-860-3875, Fax: 301-860-3887, E-mail: mie@bowiestate.edu

Lewis-Clark State College

Student Support Services TRIO Program Program Goal: Help students achieve academically and integrate into campus culture.

Program Description: The student support services TRIO program is a federally funded, student-oriented program designed to provide free academic and developmental support to enrolled students who are eligible.

Key Components: Participants enroll in four courses: English composition, public speaking, introduction to psychology, and an introductory social science course. The learning community is supported by a credited course that provides advising and develops students' writing, study, and computer skills. Participants are required to attend the *student support services* learning lab.

Evidence of Effectiveness: Data show a one-semester retention rate of 84 percent for degree-seeking provisional students accepted into the student support services program, compared with 76 percent for all provisionally accepted students.

Contact: Patricia Clyde, director, Lewis-Clark State College, Student Support Services TRIO Program, 500 8th Avenue, Lewiston, ID 83501, Telephone: 208-792-2300, FAX: 208-792-2057, E-mail: pclyde@lcsc.edu

University of Alabama

Student Support Services Program Program Goal: Increase retention and graduation rates of eligible students.

Program Description: The comprehensive federally funded TRIO program offers academic assistance to two hundred undergraduate students at the University of Alabama.

Key Components: Students receive individualized support services, including academic, career, financial, and personal counseling, advising, tutoring, and peer mentoring.

Evidence of Effectiveness: None found.

Contact: Student Support Services, 225 Osband Hall, Box 870304, Tuscaloosa, AL 35487-0304, Telephone: 205-348-7087, FAX: 205-348-5585

Arkansas State University

Upward Bound Program Program Goal: Ensure that high school students from low-income families or potential first-generation college students participate in and are successful in postsecondary education.

Program Description: The program serves seventy-five students in grades 10 to 12 who are on campus on Saturdays during the academic year and participate in a six-week summer residential program.

Key Components: The program offers secondary education students career assessment and planning, college preparation and planning, bridge programs, cultural enrichment activities, tutoring, counseling, guidance, and an on-campus residential program.

Evidence of Effectiveness: None found.

Contact: Tony Thomas, associate director of Upward Bound, P.O. Box 1390, State University, AR 72467, Telephone: 870-972-2080, Fax: 870-972-2520

Keene State College

Aspire Program Program Goal: Encourage and empower students to be self-advocates and play an active part in developing a personal academic support strategy.

Program Description: The federally funded TRIO program works closely with academic and career advising to assist students in attaining academic success.

Key Components: The program offers individualized peer tutoring, workshops in study skills, skill building, academic and financial counseling, a computer lab, and supplemental instruction.

Evidence of Effectiveness: None found.

Contact: Maria Dintino, associate director, the Elliot Center, 229 Main Street, Keene, NH 03435, Telephone: 603-358-2390, E-mail: mdintino@keene.edu

Appendix B: Annotated Bibliography

Adelman, C. (1999). *Answers in the tool box: Academic intensity, attendance patterns, and bachelor's degree attainment.* Washington, DC: Office of Education Research and Improvement, U.S. Department of Education.

This study, based on the High School and Beyond/Sophomore longitudinal database, uses both linear and logistic regression to explore the power of twenty-four variables in explaining long-term (eleven-year) bachelor's degree completion for students who attended a four-year college at any time during that period. Adelman identifies academic resources—intensity and quality of a secondary education—and continuous college enrollment as powerful predictors of degree attainment, which the author identifies as the bottom line of all postsecondary retention and persistence discussions. The comprehensive analyses of college retention literature and of an integrated national data set produced significant results for college retention policy. Adelman concludes that the true challenge of degree attainment for the higher education community requires remedying its ailing pipeline at the elementary and secondary levels.

Beil, C., Resien, C. A., and others. (1999). A longitudinal study of the effects of academic and social integration and commitment on retention. *NASPA Journal, 37*(1), 376–385.

The researchers explored the effects of academic and social integration and commitment on the persistence of first-year undergraduates at a midsize university. Empirical analysis indicated that first-semester commitment mediated the effect of early academic and social integration on persistence over time. Students' level of commitment rather than academic and social integration has a direct impact on retention. Results support the premise that early institutional adjustment is central to influencing long-term retention.

Bennett, C., and Okinaka, A. M. (1990). Factors related to persistence among Asian, black, Hispanic, and white undergraduates at a predominately white university: Comparisons between first and fourth year cohorts. *Urban Review, 23,* 33–60.

Bennett and Okinaka examined the attrition of minority and nonminority college students at Indiana University. The researchers used a revised model of black student attrition to focus on student campus life. Study findings showed white and Hispanic students who complete college are more satisfied and less alienated than African American and Asian American students who graduate. Persistence and satisfaction with campus life appear to be separate issues for African Americans and Asian Americans, however, as African Americans and Asian Americans who persisted to their fourth year of college appeared more dissatisfied with campus life than those who left the institution. These findings suggest some ethnic students who persist in college experience more trauma over time than those who drop out.

Gladieux, L. E., and Swail, W. S. (2000, May). Beyond access: Increasing the odds of college success. *Phi Delta Kappan,* pp. 688–692.

Gladieux and Swail, formerly with the College Board's policy analysis unit, briefly describe the preparation, access, and completion rates of students of various economic and racial backgrounds. They follow with a discussion of why we have not done better in opening the doors of higher education and, more important, why we have not been able to improve retention and completion rates at the postsecondary level. In the end, the authors find that improving opportunities for poor and minority students is a shared responsibility of higher education and the public sector and warn that, regardless of public policy, the solution requires hands-on, one-on-one interventions.

Gonzalez, K. P. (1999). *Campus culture and the experiences of Chicano students in predominantly white colleges and universities.* Paper prepared for the annual meeting of the Association for the Study of Higher Education, November 18–21, San Antonio, TX.

Gonzalez explored campus culture of a predominantly white metropolitan university in the Southwest to determine whether the community supported or hindered Chicano students' persistence. After observing two Chicano males for a two-year period, the researcher interpreted the study findings using three asymmetrical systems of representation: social world, physical world, and epistemological world. Research findings indicate that the two students studied felt this particular institution marginalized their culture by not completely accepting their bilingual communication styles, dress, and music, and through the absence of physical representations of their culture. In addition, the students felt the institution failed to incorporate Mexican American history and culture into educational programs. In contrast, the two students seemed to appreciate and even expand the relationships with their families and communities. Ethnic and cultural campus organizations, including Chicano faculty, Chicano literature and studies, and physical symbols, provided these students with a sense of community and pride.

Hall, C. (1999). *African American college students at a predominantly white institution: Patterns of success.* Paper prepared for an annual meeting of the Association for Institutional Research, May 30–June 2, Seattle, WA.

The study examined the interactions between students, the institution, and the external environment of successful African American students enrolled at an urban Catholic commuter university. The study used a combination of qualitative and quantitative data collection and analysis methodologies to determine how students perceived campus climate, environmental factors impeding and contributing to success, the effect of students' perceptions and expectations of the university on their experiences and knowledge, and the actions these students take to succeed academically. Research findings suggest there are more quantifiable differences between white college students and African American students who persist than between African Americans who persist and those who do not, which supports previous findings that institutional climate and other noncognitive factors are more important determinants of the academic success of African Americans than whites. Qualitative data suggest that the availability of ethnic and cultural organizations and a "critical mass" of African American students helped reduce the isolation and alienation often found on predominantly white campuses. African American coping strategies include high self-esteem, high aspirations, parental support and expectations, on-campus support (African American mentors), and involvement in cultural and ethnic organizations.

Himelhoch, C. R., Nichols, A., and others. (1997). *A comparative study of the factors which predict persistence for African American students at historically black institutions and predominantly white institutions.* Paper prepared for an annual meeting of the Association for the Study of Higher Education, November 6–9, Albuquerque, NM.

The researchers tested Bean's synthetic retention model (1982) as an accurate predictor of African American student persistence. Regression analyses of a stratified sample of the cooperative institutional research program data set for a cohort of 1986 entering freshmen and 1990 follow-up showed faculty mentoring as a predictor of African American persistence at both four-year HBCUs and predominantly white institutions. In contrast, data showed changing majors and careers as a predictor of African Americans persistence at HBCUs only. Implications for policy suggest heightening faculty-student mentoring programs at both institutional types and heightening academic and career counseling at HBCUs to affect student persistence. Further research findings are presented, and study implications are outlined.

Horn, L. J. (1998). *Undergraduates who work.* A Postsecondary Education Data Analysis Report using data from the National Postsecondary Student Aid Study (NPSAS:96). Washington, DC: National Center for Education Statistics, U.S. Department of Education.

Horn uses data from the 1996 National Postsecondary Student Aid Study to profile undergraduates who were enrolled in postsecondary institutions in the academic year 1995–96. Data analyses show that 50 percent of undergraduates in the research sample reported working to help pay for their education. Working students were employed an average of 25 hours per week, with 20 percent of full-time students also working full time. In addition, students who worked indicated that their class schedules were limited by their work schedules, and about 25 percent reported that work adversely affected their academic performance. A negative effect was found between work and one-year persistence. In addition, the data showed that students who worked a few hours per week were more likely to borrow to pay for their education than those who maintained a rigorous work schedule.

House, J. D. (1998). High school achievement and admissions test scores as predictors of course performance of Native American and Alaska native students. *Journal of Psychology, 132*(6), 680–682.

House examined the predictive relationships between admission test scores, high school achievement, and grades in specific college courses to identify factors that are predictors of Native Americans' postsecondary achievement. Using the two predictor variables of ACT composite scores and high school class percentile rank, House tracked students' grades during their first year of college. Data analyses showed significant correlations between ACT and certain courses, including chemistry, introduction to philosophy, introduction to sociology, and introduction to psychology. None of the correlations for mathematics, however, were significant. In addition, significant correlations were found for introduction to geology, introduction to sociology, and rhetoric and composition. Additional research findings are presented.

Just, H. D. (1999). *Minority retention in predominantly white universities and colleges: The importance of creating a good "fit."* (ERIC Document Reproduction Service No. ED 439 641)

Just examines retention theories and approaches for integrating students of color into predominantly white college environments. Students of color face similar college adjustment difficulties as other students. A hostile campus climate, however, further complicates their ability to integrate and adjust to campus life, ultimately influencing their college persistence. The study suggests that connection to home significantly helps students adjust to college. Just also discusses policy for aggressively recruiting culturally diverse students to create larger communities of diverse student subgroups. Similarly, recruiting minority college personnel will provide role models for students and create an environment that embraces diversity.

Kennedy, P. W., Sheckley, B. G., and others. (2000). *The dynamic nature of student persistence: Influence of interactions between student attachment, academic adaptation, and social adaptation.* Paper prepared for the annual meeting of the Association for International Research, May 21–24, Cincinnati, OH.

The researchers investigated a series of variables to determine which combination would discriminate persisters from nonpersisters after a year of college. Research findings suggest persistence is related to dynamic interactions that occur over the course of an academic year and involve students' self-evaluations. These findings are consistent with Tinto's research, which depicted persisters as students who adapted academically, improved academically over the course of the year, or achieved within their own expectations. In addition, the results support Pascarella and Terenzini's research findings that students will persist despite their academic predictions if they have successfully integrated into the campus organization. Thus, faculty should provide students with academic feedback to help them gauge academic success within a reasonable contextual framework defined by faculty; moreover, colleges and universities should provide students with continuous experiences for academic and social adaptation.

Martin, D. C., and Arendale, D. R. (1994). *Supplemental instruction: Increasing achievement and retention.* San Francisco: Jossey-Bass.

The authors describe the supplemental instruction program of the University of Missouri–Kansas City and its program development, specific goals and objectives, student and institutional outcomes, and potential for adaptation by other institutions. The program contains a number of innovative features, including identifying high-risk courses instead of high-risk students, offering assistance to every student in the high-risk courses, using leaders to conduct supplemental instruction in small group sessions, and incorporating student and faculty satisfaction surveys into measurable institutional change. The supplemental instruction program has been certified as an exemplary educational program by the U.S. Department of Education and has received national diffusion network funding.

Mortenson, T. (1998). Freshman-to-sophomore persistence rates by institutional control, academic selectivity, and degree level, 1983 to 1998. *Postsecondary Education Opportunity, 74.*

Mortenson reports on the trends and patterns of freshman-to-sophomore persistence between 1986 and 1998. Analyses of ACT data evidenced an overall decline in persistence rates, yet the results also supported previous study findings that selective private colleges enroll academically prepared high-income students who are more likely to earn degrees and open public institutions serve less academically prepared lower-income students. Although private colleges maintain higher persistence rates than public colleges, the gap is closing. This trend is attributable partly to public four-year colleges' increased academic selectivity. Enrollment persistence continues to be a challenge once students graduate from high school and enroll in college, yet the deviations for the average persistence rates, regardless of institutional type, indicate some schools are more successful at getting their freshmen to persist to the sophomore year.

Mortenson, T. (1999). Refocusing student financial aid: From grants to loans, from need to merit, from poor to affluent. *Postsecondary Education Opportunity, 82,* 1–4.

Mortenson presents a critique of federal, state, and institutional financial aid policies. Over the past two decades, policies have reversed student financial aid's original purpose of providing low-income citizens with access and equity to higher education. During the 1980s and 1990s, the federal government continued to provide middle- and high-income citizens with access to more student financial aid while restricting the financial aid specifically created to facilitate low-income citizens' college access and persistence. Mortenson contends the policy decisions were solely based on capitalism and politics and describes the practices as the "plantation economics" of higher education, where the rich get richer and the poor get poorer. Likewise, states reduced grant aid and institutions reduced need-based aid in favor of merit-based aid to attract strong academic students who would improve their college rankings. It is evident that educational opportunity is the key to private and social welfare and that society has clearly compromised the public interest by failing to help those in need.

Murdock, T. (1990). Financial aid and persistence: An integrative review of the literature. *NASPA Journal, 27*(3), 213–221.

Murdock uses meta-analysis to explore the effect of financial aid on student persistence among different student groups and across types of institutions. Data analyses indicated that financial aid was an important factor affecting and promoting persistence among minority groups. In addition, the dollar amount of financial aid had a significant positive effect on persistence. The researcher also found a stronger effect for private institutions than for public ones.

Nagda, B. A., Gregerman, S. R., and others. (1998). Undergraduate student-faculty research partnerships affect student retention. *Review of Higher Education, 22*(1), 55–72.

This study assessed the effect of the University of Michigan's Undergraduate Research Opportunity Program, which brokered intellectual relationships between faculty and first-year students and sophomores as a step in student retention. Based on retention frameworks, which advocate student college integration, the researchers used a participant–control group research design. Research findings indicated partnerships (student-faculty and student-student) are successful in promoting retention of some students. Specifically, the program increased the retention of participating African American students and African American students with lower academic achievement. These findings are consistent with previous research that showed integration is critical to underrepresented minority students at PWIs, specifically African Americans. The effects were less significant for white and Hispanic students. The authors suggest the challenge of integration may be different for Hispanic students than for African American students, particularly as most Hispanic students attending the institution resided out of state and may have experienced deeper feelings of isolation as a result of the absence of immediate family support.

Native American Higher Education Consortium. (2000). *Creating role models for change: A survey of tribal college graduates.* Alexandria, VA: Native American Higher Education Consortium.

This study surveyed tribal college graduates to assess their fundamental characteristics. Descriptive analyses indicate average tribal college graduates are nontraditional female, first-generation Native Americans who receive associate degrees and certificates and remain in the local community upon graduation. Many of these graduates also have dependents under the age of 18. The average graduate majored in more vocational and technical fields such as business, health care, computer technology, education, and human services. Many tribal college graduates are employed in or continue to enroll in postsecondary courses, and some even transition to predominantly white institutions. Because tribal colleges enroll only about 600 students, on average, the classes are small, allowing faculty more time to cultivate and mentor students. Although tribal college graduates clearly earned higher salaries as a result of attaining a postsecondary degree, these graduates still earned much less than the national average of those in similar fields. Approximately 80 percent of tribal college graduates were satisfied with their academic higher educational experiences; however, they were less satisfied with the institutions' facilities and equipment. Like HBCUs, tribal colleges seem to have a distinct role in the higher education community of successfully providing Native Americans with postsecondary education.

Pavel, D. M., Skinner, R. R., and others. (1999, Spring). Native Americans and Alaska Natives in postsecondary education. *Education Statistics Quarterly, 1*(1), 67–74.

Statistical analyses compare data of Native Americans involved in postsecondary education with the general population of postsecondary students. The Native American population has significantly increased from about two hundred thirty-seven thousand recorded in 1970 to slightly under two million in 1990. Proportionally, Native Americans make up 0.08 percent of the population. Some of the growth is attributable to the self-identification by individuals as Native Americans. Research indicates that although Native Americans have made substantial gains since the 1970s, they still lag behind the general population in college attendance, persistence, and completion. Native American students are more likely to be first-generation, low-income students; 62 percent of students enrolled depend on student financial aid to pay for college. They are also less likely to receive academic preparation for college than the overall students. The majority of Native Americans attending college, 87 percent, attend two-year and public institutions, compared with 78 percent of all students. The number of Native American females attending college has increased noticeably (52 percent) since 1970. College enrollments are concentrated in areas with high Native American populations, principally western states such as New Mexico, Oklahoma, and Arizona.

Redd, K. E. (2000). *Discounting toward disaster: Tuition discounting, college finances, and enrollments of low-income undergraduates.* Indianapolis: USA Group Foundation.

To examine the effects of college tuition discounting, Redd compared data from annual institutional student aid surveys of private colleges and universities with enrollment and Pell Grant data from the U.S. Department of

Education. Data analyses indicated that (1) at least one-fourth of the colleges and universities used discounting strategies that resulted in large losses of tuition revenue; (2) institutions with the greatest increases in discount rates raised their spending on institutional grants by $3,375 per undergraduate, but their tuition and fee revenue grew by just $3,069; (3) discounting strategies do not appear to have significantly improved the academic profiles of admitted undergraduates when measured by changes in median admission test scores of entering first-year students; (4) tuition discounting does appear to have helped institutions increase their numbers of low-income undergraduates; and (5) the increased use of tuition discounting does appear to have made it possible for more students from all income levels to enter higher education.

Rodriguez, A. L., Guido-DiBrito, F., and others. (2000). Latina college students: Issues and challenges for the 21st century. *NASPA Journal, 37*(3), 511–527.

This article discusses the barriers to Latina participation in higher education, factors contributing to the success of high-achieving Latinas, and strategies for student and academic affairs administrators to promote the success of Latina students. The Latino population remains one of the most underrepresented groups in the higher education system, which can be traced to Latinos' low socioeconomic status. Barriers facing Latinas in postsecondary education include cultural stereotyping; financial, academic, and social stresses; and institutional marginalization. To support the success of Latinas in higher education, institutions should provide adequate and realistic financial aid that includes more grants and scholarships than loans, offer more academic support to integrate students academically, provide more social and cultural support systems that value the Latina culture, and create a campus that embraces diversity.

St. John, E. P., Paulsen, M. B., and others. (1996). The nexus between college choice and persistence. *Research in Higher Education, 37*(2), 175–220.

Initial college choices are considered an influence on persistence, but the impact of students' choices has seldom been considered in studying their persistence and student outcomes. According to these researchers, two distinct sets of theories and research have evolved regarding college choice and persistence as a result of considering them as two separate managerial functions in higher education. College choice research often supports marketing and recruitment, while persistence research supports student retention and completion. Using data from the national postsecondary student aid study, this study examined the influence of finance-related reasons for college choice on persistence decisions. Data showed that finance-related choices had direct and indirect influences on college persistence and that market-based monetary measures of financial aid, tuition, housing costs, and other living costs had substantial direct effects on persistence.

Smedley, B. D., Myers, H. F., and others. (1993). Minority-status stresses and the college adjustment of ethnic minority freshmen. *Journal of Higher Education, 64*(4), 434–452.

Nonwhite students attending PWIs are likely to view these campuses as hostile, alienating, socially isolating, and less responsive to their needs and interests. This study confirmed the hypothesis that minority status stress confers an additional risk to the academic adjustment of nonwhite students beyond those normally experienced by white students. The researchers proposed a multidimensional stress-coping model of individual characteristics that moderate or enhance a student's vulnerability to academic failure, psychological and cultural stresses students encounter during their academic careers, and students' coping strategies, all important in nonwhite college students' adjustment and achievement. Chronic strains associated with being a student and life events are important correlates of psychological distress in nonwhite freshmen, and minority status stresses make a substantial additional contribution to this correlation. Research also supported previous findings that regardless of the sources of stress, they are not as important as academic preparation when accounting for present academic achievement.

Stewart, G. L., Russell, R. B., and others. (1997). The comprehensive role of student affairs in African American student retention. *Journal of College Admission, 154,* 6–11.

The authors contend that student affairs personnel and professionals concerned with the matriculation and retention of minority students must be aware of the need to create an accepting and supportive atmosphere for African American students at PWIs. They discuss developing a supportive campus using a series of concepts and interventions, including precollegiate outreach, orientation, academic advising, tutoring, career planning and placement, financial aid, residential life, and structured student activities

Strage, A. A. (1999). Social and academic integration and college success: Similarities and differences as a function of ethnicity and family educational background. *College Student Journal, 33*(2), 198–205.

Strage examined college students' social and academic integration and college persistence to discern similarities and differences among cultural and educational subgroups of the "new" college-going population—more students of color, part-part-timers, and older students. Data analyses of psychosocial survey responses show differences in students' social and academic integration by cultural subgroups. White and Hispanic students were slightly more confident in their academic abilities and much more socially confident than Asian American students. They felt that they had better rapport with instructors, and they reported more internal locus of control. No significant differences were found between first- and later-generation students for academic and social integration. The relationship between grades and academic and social integration was much weaker than the relationship between achievement and motivation and integration. Academic confidence, leadership, and teacher rapport were positively correlated with persistence for whites. Academic confidence and teacher rapport were predictive of persistence for Asian Americans. Academic confidence and locus of control were significantly correlated with persistence for Hispanics.

Swail, W. S. (2000). Preparing America's disadvantaged for college: Programs that increase college opportunity. In Cabrera and S. M. La Nasa (Eds.), *Understanding the college choice of disadvantaged students.* New Directions for Institutional Research, No. 107. San Francisco: Jossey-Bass.

This chapter uses selected indicators from the national survey of precollege outreach programs to describe how these programs work within the scheme of public schooling in America. The author describes the importance of education to lifting the minds, spirits, and opportunities of our less-advantaged youth and how early intervention programs can be a primary tool to make it happen. The chapter concludes with four points on how to alter public policy to improve the practice of early outreach efforts.

Swail, W. S., and Perna, L. W. (2002). Pre-college outreach programs: A national perspective. In W. Tierney and L. Hagedorn (Eds.), *Increasing access to college*. Albany: State University of New York Press.

This chapter uses data from the national survey of precollege outreach programs to describe the landscape of programs in operation around the United States. Included in this review are discussions of funding, location, types of interventions, staffing, and size of programs. The chapter begins with a brief discussion of federal and nongovernmental programs to increase access for underrepresented students and concludes with ten viewpoints collected during focus groups with program directors from around the country for improving program services and stability.

Terenzini, P. T., Cabrera, A. F., and others. (2001). *Swimming against the tide: The poor in American higher education*. New York: College Entrance Examination Board.

This report presents profiles of low-income college students and the nature of their collegiate experience. Low-income students are likely to be nonwhite, have parents with high school diplomas or less, come from single-family homes, make decisions to attend college without parental guidance, attend public two-year institutions, and have limited academic resources. Low-income students are equally involved in academics as high-income students but significantly less involved in out-of-class campus activities. Although financial considerations are important to facilitate students' enrollment and persistence in college, they do not fully explain why low-income students attend and persist in higher education.

Terenzini, P. T., Springer, L., and others. (1996). First-generation college students: Characteristics, experiences, and cognitive development. *Research in Higher Education, 37*(1), 1–22.

This study compares the characteristics and college experiences of first-generation students with those of traditional students to determine any differences between the groups and the educational impacts of the differences to address the increasing numbers enrolling in higher education. The conceptual model posits six sets of constructs defining a causal sequence that begins when students enter college with an array of academic resources. The precollege characteristics are presumed to influence students' course-taking patterns, formal classroom experiences, and out-of-class experiences during college, which ultimately influence educational outcomes. The researchers used first-year student data collected as part of a three-year longitudinal national survey of precollege characteristics, a cognitive assessment instrument, and a college experience questionnaire. Research findings of precollege characteristics showed first-generation students were more likely to come from low-income families, to be Hispanic, to have weaker cognitive skills (reading, math, and critical thinking), to have lower degree aspirations, and to have been less involved with peers and teachers while in high school. Research findings also indicated that hours spent studying positively impacted first-generation students' gains in reading skills during their first year, which suggests a need to increase these students' study time, possibly through study groups, peer tutoring, and financial assistance to reduce students' off-campus work hours.

Thayer, P. B. (2000). Retention of students from first generation and low income backgrounds. *Opportunity Outlook.*

Based on theoretical models of retention, Thayer presents critical analyses of the characteristics of first-generation and low-income students, their challenges to higher education, and programming that supports their postsecondary participation. Thayer offers a dual strategic approach for facilitating the attainment of a college degree, which consists of admissions selection and student support components. His discussion of student support services centers on integrating students into the academic and social structures of institutions. Thayer expects these strategies to provide increased higher education opportunities for low-income and first-generation students. Although the recommended strategies are targeted to at-risk students, they are applicable to all college student populations.

Tinto, V. (1975). Dropout from higher education: A theoretical synthesis of recent research. *Review of Higher Education, 45*(1), 89–125.

Tinto's landmark theoretical model provides the framework for numerous college student retention studies. It posits that student-institution fit shapes students' goal commitment and commitment to the institution, which ultimately influences student persistence. The model explores the multifaceted functioning of interactions between the student and the college academic and social systems on student persistence. Although the model failed to address in detail the effect of external campus factors, such as finances, family obligations, and external peer groups on students' persistence, it has remained the foundation of student retention studies and practice for more than twenty-five years.

Volle, K., and Federico, A. (1997). *Missed opportunities: A look at disadvantaged college aspirants.* Boston: Education Resource Institute.

Volle and Federico examined three factors that significantly influence college access, persistence, and degree attainment of some first-generation and divorced students on welfare. Although students in these subgroups face barriers unique to each subgroup, financial and academic limitations hinder degree attainment across subgroups. The authors recommend investing in early intervention and precollege programs, increasing availability of college awareness information, increasing availability of support services, promoting greater consistency and clarity in financial aid policies regarding parental contributions to college, and lessening restrictions prohibiting welfare recipients from participating in college.

Wallace, D., Abel, R., and others. (2000). Clearing a path for success: Deconstructing borders through undergraduate mentoring. *Review of Educational Research, 24*(1), 87–102.

The researchers use qualitative research methodology to examine the effectiveness of formal mentoring programs for high-risk undergraduates at a southern comprehensive, four-year regional university. Formal mentoring was defined as a deliberate matching of university personnel with high-risk students, a group that may include nonwhite, female, low-income, physically challenged, and first-generation college students. Study findings indicate that formal mentoring appeared to positively affect student participation, retention, and success in college. Students who had been involved with student support services, Veterans Upward Bound, and the educational opportunity center reported commitment to continuing their education as a result of support personnel's counseling, tutoring, and guidance.

References

Adelman, C. (1996, Oct. 4). The truth about remedial work. *Chronicle of Higher Education.*

Adelman, C. (1997, Oct. 22). Turn college "access" into "participation." *Education Week on the Web.* [http://www.edweek.org].

Adelman, C. (1999). *Answers in the tool box: Academic intensity, attendance patterns, and bachelor's degree attainment.* Jessup, MD: Office of Educational Research and Improvement, U.S. Department of Education.

Adelman, C. (2002). The relationship between urbanicity and educational outcomes. In W. G. Tierney and L. S. Hagedorn (Eds.), *Increasing access to college: Extending possibilities for all students* (pp. 35–64). Albany, NY: State University of New York Press.

Advisory Committee on Student Financial Assistance. (2001). *Access denied: Restoring the nation's commitment to equal education opportunity.* Washington, DC: Advisory Committee on Student Financial Assistance.

Ajzen, I., and Fishbein, M. (1972). Attitudes and normative beliefs as factors influencing behavioral intentions. *Journal of Personality and Social Psychology, 21*(2), 1–9.

Ajzen, I., and Fishbein, M. (1977). Attitude-behavior relations: A theoretical analysis and review of empirical research. *Psychological Bulletin, 84*(5), 888–918.

Alexander, K. L., Pallas, A. M., and Holupka, S. (1987). Consistency and change in educational stratification: Recent trends regarding social background and college access. *Research in Social Stratification and Mobility, 6,* 161–185.

Allen, D. (1994). *The Iliad and the Odyssey of student attrition.* Paper presented at the Association for Institutional Research, May 30, New Orleans, LA.

Alliance for Equity in Higher Education (2001). Remarks at the meeting of the Lumina Foundation for Education regarding the status of minorities in higher education, Oct.

Alwin, W. F., and Otto, L. B. (1977). High school context effects on aspirations. *Sociology of Education, 50,* 259–273.

American Council on Education. (2000). *2000 status report on the Pell Grant program.* Washington, DC: American Council on Education.

American River College. (2001). *Beacon program: Peer-assisted learning.* Retrieved Dec. 18, 2001. [http://www.arc.losrios.cc.ca.us/learnres/beacon.html].

Ancis, J. R., Sedlacek, W. E., and Mohr, J. J. (2000). Student perceptions of campus cultural climate by race. *Journal of Counseling and Development, 78*(2), 180–185.

Anderson, B. T. (1989). Black participation and performance in high school. In W. Pearson, Jr., and H. K. Bechtel (Eds.) *Blacks, Science, and American Education.* New Brunswick, NJ: Rutgers University Press.

Anderson, E. (1985). Forces influencing student persistence and achievement. In L. Noel, R. S. Levitze, and D. Saluri (Eds.), *Increasing student retention* (pp. 44–61). San Francisco: Jossey-Bass.

Arrington, P. G. (1994). *AASCU/Sallie Mae national retention project.* Washington, DC: American Association of State Colleges and Universities.

Association of American Medical Colleges (1992). *Project 3000 by 2000.* Technical assistance manual: Guidelines for action. Washington, DC: AAMC.

Astin, A. W. (1975). *Preventing students from dropping out.* San Francisco: Jossey-Bass.

Astin, A. W. (1977). *Four critical years.* San Francisco: Jossey-Bass.

Astin, A. W. (1982). *Minorities in American higher education: Recent trends, current prospects, and recommendations.* San Francisco: Jossey-Bass.

Astin, A. W. (1987). Competition or cooperation? Teaching teamwork as a basic skill. *Change, 19*(5), 12–19.

Astin, A. W. (1993a). What matters in college: Four critical years revisited (1st ed.). San Francisco, CA: Jossey-Bass.

Astin, A. W. (1993b). Diversity and multiculturalism on campus: How are students affected? *Change, 25*(2), Mar–Apr, 44–49.

Bakst, D. (2000). Race-targeted financial aid: Untangling the legal web. *Student Aid Transcript, 11*(2), 4–8.

Beal, P. E., and Noel, L. (1980). *What works in student retention.* Iowa City, IA: American College Testing Program.

Bean, J. P. (1982). *Student attrition, intentions, and confidence.* New Directions for Higher Education, no. 17, pp. 291–320. San Francisco: Jossey-Bass.

Bean, J. P. (1986). Assessing and reducing attrition. In D. Hossler (Ed.), *Managing college enrollment* (pp. 47–61). San Francisco: Jossey-Bass.

Bean, J. P., and Eaton, S. B. (2000). A psychological model of college student retention. In J. M. Braxton (Ed.), *Reworking the student departure puzzle.* Nashville: Vanderbilt University Press.

Bean, L. (2001). Court rules against affirmative action at University of Georgia. *Diversity Inc.* [http://www.diversityinc.com/public/1301.cfm]. Accessed Oct. 29, 2003.

Beil, C., Resien, C. A., and Zea, M. C. (1999). A longitudinal study of the effects of academic and social integration and commitment on retention. *NASPA Journal, 37*(1), 376–385.

Bennett, C., and Okinaka, A. M. (1990). Factors related to persistence among Asian, black, Hispanic, and white undergraduates as a predominately white university: Comparisons between first and fourth year cohorts. *Urban Review, 23,* 33–60.

Bentler, P. M., and Speckart, G. (1979). Models of attitude-behavior relations. *Psychological Review, 86*(5), 452–464.

Bentler, P. M., and Speckart, G. (1981). Attitudes "cause" behaviors: A structural equation analysis. *Journal of Personality and Social Psychology, 40*(2), 226–238.

Berg, J. H., and Peplau, L. A. (1982). Loneliness: The relationship of self-disclosure and androgyny. *Personality and Social Psychology Bulletin, 8,* 524–630.

Berkner, L., and Chavez, L. (1997). *Access to postsecondary education for the 1992 high school graduates* (NCES 98–105). Washington, DC: National Center for Education Statistics, U.S. Department of Education.

Berkner, L., He, S., Cataldi, E. F., and Knepper, P. (2002). *Descriptive summary of 1995–96 beginning postsecondary students: Six years later.* Washington, DC: U.S. Department of Education, Institute of Education Sciences. (NCES 2003-151)

Berryman, S. E. (1983). *Who will do science? Trends, and their causes in minority and female representation among holders of advanced degrees in science and mathematics. A special report.* ERIC Document Reproduction Service No. ED245052.

Bird, T. (1990). The school teacher's portfolio: An essay on possibilities. In J. Millman and L. Darling-Hammond (Eds.), *The new handbook of teacher evaluation* (pp. 241–256). Newbury Park, CA: Sage.

Blanchette, C. M. (1994). *Higher education grants effective at increasing minorities' chances of graduating.* Washington, DC: Health, Education, and Human Services Division, General Accounting Office.

Borman, G. D., Stringfield, S., and Rachuba, L. (2000). *Advancing minority high achievement: National trends and promising practices.* New York: College Board.

Bowen, H. R. (1980). *Adult learning, higher education, and the economics of unused capacity.* Direction Papers in Lifelong Learning. Princeton, NJ: College Board.

Bowen, H. R. (1997). *Investment in learning: The individual and social value of American higher education.* Baltimore: Johns Hopkins University Press.

Bowie State University. (1995). *Model institutions for excellence initiative: Bowie State University science, engineering, and mathematics education reform.* Retrieved from the World Wide Web Jan. 5, 2002.

Braxton, J. M., and Lien, L. A. (2000). The viability of academic integration as a central construct in Tinto's interactionalist theory of college student departure. In J. M. Braxton (Ed.), *Reworking the student departure puzzle* (pp. 11–28). Nashville, TN: Vanderbilt University Press.

Brower, A. M. (1992). The "second half" of student integration: The effects of life task predominance on student persistence. *Journal of Higher Education, 63*(4), 441–462.

Brunner, B. (2002). *Timeline of affirmative action milestones.* Learning Network Web site. Retrieved Aug. 13, 2003. [http://www.infoplease.com/spot/affirmativetimeline1.html].

Cabrera, A. F., Castaneda, M. B., Nora, A., and Hengstler, D. (1992). The convergence between two theories of college persistence. *Journal of Higher Education, 63*(2), 143–164.

Cabrera, A. F., Nora, A., and Castaneda, M. B. (1992). The role of finances in the persistence process: A structural model. *Research in Higher Education, 33*(5), 571–593.

Cabrera, A. F., Nora, A., and Castaneda, M. B. (1993). College persistence: Structured equation modeling test of an integrated model of student retention. *Journal of Higher Education, 64*(2), 123–139.

Cabrera, A. F., and La Nasa, S. M. (2000). Three critical tasks America's disadvantaged face on their path to college. In A. F. Cabrera and S. M. La Nasa (Eds.), *Understanding the college choice of disadvantaged students. New Directions for Institutional Research,* no. 107. San Francisco, CA: Jossey-Bass.

Cabrera, A. F., La Nasa, S. M., and Burkam, K. R. (2001). *Pathways to a four-year degree: The higher education story of one generation.* Unpublished report.

Capella, B., Hetzler, J., and MacKenzie, C. (1983). The effects of positive peer influence on study habits. *Reading Improvements, 20*(4), 229–302.

Chickering, A. W. (1974). *Commuting versus resident students: Overcoming the educational inequities of living off campus.* San Francisco: Jossey-Bass.

Christman, D. E. (2000). Multiple realities: Characteristics of loan defaulters at a two-year public institution. *Community College Review, 27*(4), 16–32.

Clayton, M. (2001). Michigan affirmative action case will reverberate widely. *Christian Science Monitor.* Retrieved Aug. 13, 2003. [http://www.csmonitor.com/2001/1023/p14s1-leca.html].

Clewell, B., and Ficklen, M. (1986). *Improving minority retention in higher education: A search for effective institutional practices.* Princeton, NJ: Educational Testing Service.

Cohen, R. (2002, Jan. 17). A negative impression on affirmative action. *Washington Post,* p. A23.

College Board. (2001a). Data from 2001 college-bound seniors cohort. Retrieved Aug. 13, 2003. [http://www.collegeboard.com]

College Board. (2001b). *Trends in student aid 2001.* Washington, DC: College Board.

College Board. (2002). *Trends in student aid 2002.* Washington, DC: College Board.

Collison, M. (1988). Complex application form discourages many students from applying for federal financial aid. *Chronicle of Higher Education,* A19, A30.

Cope, R., and Hannah, W. (1975). *Revolving college doors: The causes and consequences of dropping out, stopping out, and transferring.* New York: Wiley.

Couch, R., and Holmes, B. (1997, Fall). Seamless collaboration for student success: Effective strategies for retaining minority students. *Michigan Community College Journal: Research and Practice, 3*(2), 43–51.

Cunningham, A. F., and O'Brien, C. (1999). *Do grants matter? Student grant aid and affordability.* Washington, DC: Institute for Higher Education Policy.

Davies, G. (2001, Nov. 30). Higher education is a public health issue. *Chronicle of Higher Education,* p. B16.

Dreisbach, M., and Keogh, B. K. (1982). Testwiseness as a factor in readiness: Test performance of young Mexican-American children. *Journal of Educational Psychology, 74*(2), 224–229.

Eaton, S. B., and Bean, J. P. (1995). An approach/avoidance behavioral model of college student attrition. *Research in Higher Education, 36*(6), 617–645.

Ekstrom, R. B. (1991). *Attitudes toward borrowing and participation in post-secondary education.* Paper presented at the annual meeting of the Association for the Study of Higher Education, Oct. 31–Nov. 3, Boston, MA.

Elam, J. C. (1989). *Blacks in higher education: Overcoming the odds.* Lanham, MD: University Press of America.

Endo, J., and Harpel, R. (1982). The effects of student-faculty interaction on students' educational outcomes. *Research in Higher Education, 16,* 115–135.

Epps, A. C. (1979). Summer programs for undergraduates in a professional medical educational environment. In *Medical Education: Responses to a Challenge.* Mount Kisco, NY: Futura.

Feagin, J. R., and Sikes, M. P. (1995, summer). How black students cope with racism on white campuses. *Journal of Blacks in Higher Education, 8,* 91–97.

Fenske, R. H., Porter, J. D., and DuBrock, C. P. (2000). Tracking financial aid and persistence of women, minority, and needy students in science, engineering and mathematics. *Research in Higher Education, 41*(1), 67–94.

Fernandez, Y. M., Whitlock, E. R., Maring, C., and VanEarden, K. (1998). *Evaluation of a first-year pilot program for academically underrepresented students at a private liberal arts college.* Amherst: University of Massachusetts.

Fiske, E. B. (1988). The undergraduate Hispanic experience: A case of juggling two cultures. *Change, 20*(3), 29–33.

Flannery, J., and others. (1973). *Final report from the ad hoc committee to study attrition at Miami-Dade Community College, North Campus.* Miami: Miami-Dade Junior College.

Flores, M. (2003, Aug. 8). UT get ready to wade into affirmative action: School system given go-ahead for new policies. *San Antonio Epress-News,* p. 1A.

Forrest, A. (1982). *Increasing student competence and persistence: The best case for general education.* Iowa City: American College Testing Program, National Center for Advancement of Educational Practices.

Franklin, J. (1988). The desperate need for black teachers. *Educational Digest, 53*(7), 14–15.

Fullilove, R. E., and Treisman, P. U. (1990). Mathematics achievement among African American undergraduates at the University of California, Berkeley: An evaluation of the mathematics workshop program. *Journal of Negro Education, 59*(3), 463–478.

Gladieux, L. E. (2001). Unpublished paper. Toronto: Canada Millennium Scholarship Foundation.

Gladieux, L. E., and Swail, W. S. (1998). Postsecondary education: Student success, not just access. In S. Halperin (Ed.), *The forgotten half revisited—1998* (pp. 101–114). Washington, DC: American Youth Policy Forum.

Gladieux, L. E., and Wolanin, T. (1976). *Congress and the colleges: The national politics of higher education.* Lexington, MA: D. C. Heath.

Gonzalez, K. P. (1999). *Campus culture and the experiences of Chicano students in predominantly white colleges and universities.* Paper presented at the annual meeting of the Association for the Study of Higher Education, Nov. 18–21, San Antonio, TX.

Griffen, O. T. (1992). The impacts of academic and social integration for black students in higher education. In M. Lang and C. Ford (Eds.), *Strategies for retaining minority students in higher education.* Springfield, IL: Charles C. Thomas Publishers.

Guinier, L. (2001, Dec. 14). Colleges should take "confirmative action" in admissions. *Chronicle of Higher Education.*

Hall, C. (1999). *African American college students at a predominantly white institution: Patterns of success.* Paper presented at the annual meeting of the Association for Institutional Research, May 30–June 2, Seattle, WA.

Halpern, D. (1992). A cognitive approach to improving thinking skills in the sciences and mathematics. In D. Halpern, D. (Ed.), *Enhancing thinking skills in the sciences and mathematics* (pp. 1–14). Hillsdale, NY: Lawrence Erlbaum Associates.

Heller, D. E. (1999). Institutional need-based and non-need grants: Trends and differences among college and university sectors. *Journal of Student Financial Aid, 29*(3), 7–24.

Heller, D. E. (2001a). *The effects of tuition process and financial aid on enrollment in higher education.* Rancho Cordova, CA: EdFund.

Heller, D. E. (2001b). Race, gender, and institutional financial aid awards. *Journal of Student Financial Aid, 31*(1), 7–24.

Heller, D. E., and Rasmussen, C. J. (2001). *Merit scholarships and college access: Evidence from two states.* Paper presented to the State Merit Aid Programs: College Access and Equity Conference sponsored by the Civil Rights Project, Dec., Harvard University.

Hentoff, N. (1997). *Cheryl Hopwood v. State of Texas.* Retrieved Aug. 13, 2003. [http://www.villagevoice.com/issues/9747/hentoff.php].

Himelhoch, C. R., Nichols, A., Ball, S. R., and Black, L. C. (1997). *A comparative study of the factors which predict persistence for African American students at historically black institutions and predominantly white institutions.* Paper presented at the annual meeting of the Association for the Study of Higher Education, Nov. 6–9, Albuquerque, NM.

Horn, L. (1998). *Undergraduates who work.* Postsecondary Education Descriptive Analysis Reports. Statistical Analysis Report. Washington, DC: National Center for Education Statistics, U.S. Department of Education.

Horn, L., and Kojaku, L. (2001). *High school academic curriculum and the persistence path through college.* (Report No. NCES 2001-163). Washington, DC: U.S. Department of Education, Office of Educational Research and Improvement.

Horn, L., and Maw, C. (1994). *Undergraduates who work while enrolled in postsecondary education: 1989–90.* Postsecondary Education Descriptive Analysis Reports. Statistical Analysis Report. Washington, DC: National Center for Education Statistics, U.S. Department of Education.

Hossler, D. (1984). *Enrollment management.* New York: College Entrance Examination Board.

Hossler, D., Braxton, J., and Coopersmith, G. (1989). Understanding student college choice. In John Smart (Ed.), *Higher education: Handbook of theory and research* (vol. V, pp. 231–288). New York: Agathon Press.

Hossler, D., Schmit, J., and Vesper, N. (1999). *Going to college: How social, economic, and educational factors influence the decisions students make.* Baltimore: Johns Hopkins University Press.

Hyman, A. K. (1988). Group work as a teaching strategy in black student retention in higher education. In M. Lang and C. Ford (Eds.), *Black student retention in higher education.* Springfield, IL: Charles C. Thomas Publishers.

Institute for Higher Education Policy (1998). *Reaping the benefits: Defining the public and private value of going to college.* Washington, DC: IHEP.

Jencks, C., and Phillips, M. (1998). *The black-white test score gap.* Washington, DC: Brookings Institution.

Just, H. D. (1999). *Minority retention in predominantly white universities and colleges: The importance of creating a good "fit."* (ED 439 641)

Justiz, Manuel (1994). Demographic trends and the challenges to American higher education. In Justiz, Wilson, and Bjork (Eds.), *Minorities in Higher Education* (pp. 1–21). Phoenix, AZ: Oryz Press and ACE.

Kalechstein, P., and others (1981). The effects of instruction on test-taking skills in second grade children. *Measurement and evaluation in guidance, 13*(4), 198–201.

Kanter, R. M. (1983). *The change masters: Innovation for productivity in the American corporation.* New York: Simon & Schuster.

Kennedy, P. W., Sheckley, B. G., and Kehrhahn, M. T. (2000). *The dynamic nature of student persistence: Influence of interactions between student attachment, academic adaptation, and social adaptation.* Paper presented at the annual meeting of the Association for International Research, May 21–24, Cincinnati, OH.

King, J. E. (1999). *Money matters: The impact of race/ethnicity and gender on how students pay for college.* Washington, DC: American Council on Education.

Lane, C. (2003, June 24). Affirmative action for diversity is upheld in 5 to 4 vote: Justices approve U. Mich. Law School Plan. *Washington Post,* p. A1.

Lenning, O. T. (1982). Variable-selection and measurement concerns. In E. T. Pascarella (Ed.), *Studying student attrition.* San Francisco: Jossey-Bass.

Lenning, O. T., Beal, P. E., and Sauer, K. (1980). *Retention and attrition: Evidence for action and research.* Boulder, CO: National Center for Higher Education Management Systems.

Leslie, L. L., and Brinkman, P. T. (1988). *The economic value of higher education.* New York: Macmillan.

Levey, R. A. (2003). Discriminate but obfuscate: The court's message to universities. *National Review Online.* [http://www.nationalreview.com/comment/comment-levy062703.asp]. Accessed Oct. 29, 2003.

Levine, A., and Nidiffer, J. (1996). *Beating the odds: How the poor get to college.* San Francisco: Jossey-Bass.

Levitze, R. S., and Noel, L. (1985). Using a systematic approach to assessing retention needs. In L. Noel, R. S. Levitze, D. Saluri, and Associates (Eds.), *Increasing student retention.* San Francisco: Jossey-Bass.

Liu, R., and Liu, E. (2000). Institutional integration: An analysis of Tinto's theory. Paper presented at the AIR Forum, Cincinnati, OH.

Lum, L. (1997). *Difference of opinion about* Hopwood. *Houston Chronicle.* [http://www.chron.com/content/chronicle/page1/97/03/26/hopwood.2–0.html]

Lynch, M. W. (2001). *Ward Connerly's new cause: The man who ended affirmative action in California is pushing for a colorblind government.* Retrieved Aug. 13, 2003. [http://www.reason.com/ml/ml053101.shtml].

Malcom, S. M. (1983). *Equity and excellence: Compatible goals.* Washington, DC: American Association for the Advancement of Science.

Martin, A.D.J. (1985). Financial aid. In L. Noel, R. S. Levitze, D. Saluri, and Associates (Eds.), *Increasing student retention.* San Francisco: Jossey-Bass.

Matyas, M. L. (1991). Women, minorities, and persons with physical disabilities in science and engineering: Contributing factors and study methodology. In M. L. Matyas (Ed.), *Investing in human potential: Science and engineering at the crossroads* (pp. 13–36). Washington, DC: American Association for the Advancement of Science.

McDermott, L. C., Piternick, L. K., and Rosenquist, M. (1980, Jan.). Helping minority students succeed in science. *Journal of College Science Teaching, 9*(3), 135–140.

McPherson, M. S. (1993). How can we tell if financial aid is working? In M. S. McPherson, M. O. Schapiro, and G. C. Winston (Eds.), *Paying the piper: Productivity, incentives, and financing in U.S. higher education.* Ann Arbor: University of Michigan Press.

Mendoza, J., and Corzo, M. (1996). *Tracking/monitoring program to enhance multicultural student retention.* Paper presented at the Consortium for Community College Development's Annual Summer Institute, June 23–26, Charleston, SC.

Merisotis, J., and O'Brien, C. T. (1998). *Minority-serving institutions: Distinct purposes, common goals.* New Directions for Higher Education, no. 102. San Francisco: Jossey-Bass.

Metzner, B. S., and Bean, J. P. (1987). The estimation of a conceptual model of nontraditional undergraduate student attrition. *Research in Higher Education, 27*(1), 15–38.

Moline, A. E. (1987). Financial aid and student persistence: An application of causal modeling. *Research in Higher Education, 26*(2), 130–147.

Mooney, C. (1988). The college president. *Chronicle of Higher Education, 34*(29), 14–16.

Moore, W. J., and Carpenter, L. C. (1985). Academically underprepared students. In L. Noel, R. S. Levitze, D. Saluri, and Associates (Eds.), *Increasing student retention* (pp. 95–115). San Francisco: Jossey-Bass.

Mortenson, T. G. (2001a). College continuation rates for recent high school graduates, 1959 to 2000. *Postsecondary Education Opportunity, 107,* 1–10.

Mortenson, T. G. (2001b). College participation by family income, gender, and race/ethnicity for dependent 18 to 24 year olds, 1996 to 2000. *Postsecondary Education Opportunity, 114,* 1–8.

Mortenson, T. G. (2001c). Trends in college participation by family income, 1970 to 1999. *Postsecondary Education Opportunity, 106,* 1–8.

Mortenson, T. (2002). *Higher education as private and social investment.* Presentation to the Key Bank Financing Conference, Feb. 15, Orlando, FL.

Mortenson, T. G., and Wu, Z. (1990). *High school graduation and college participation of young adults by family income backgrounds, 1970 to 1989.* ACT Student Financial Aid Research Report No. 90–3. Iowa City: ACT Educational and Social Research.

Mumper, M. (1996). Beyond financial aid: Alternative approaches to improving college participation. *Review of Educational Research, 22,* 83–97.

Murdock, T. (1990). Financial aid and persistence: An integrative review of the literature. *NASPA Journal, 27*(3), 213–221.

Murphy, S. J., and Fath, K. Q. (1996). *Successful implementation of comprehensive support services and its effect on student retention.* Consortium for Student Retention Data Exchange. Retrieved Dec. 18, 2001. [http://www.occe.ou.edu/CSRDE/1996.htm].

Myers, K. A., and Birk, N. A. (1998). *First-year learning team (FLighT) program.* Consortium for Student Retention Data Exchange. Retrieved Dec. 18, 2001. [http://www.occe.ou.edu/CSRDE/1998.htm]

National Association of State Student Grant and Aid Programs. (2001). *31st annual survey report, 1999–2000 academic year.* Albany: National Association of State Student Grant and Aid Programs.

National Resource Center for the First-Year Experience and Students in Transition. (1999). *Research on University 101: Assessment of outcome.* Retrieved from the World Wide Web Jan. 3, 2002.

National Collegiate Athletic Association. (2000). *Graduation-rates report, all divisions.* Indianapolis: National Collegiate Athletic Association.

National Collegiate Athletic Association. (2001a). *2000 Division I graduation-rates report.* Indianapolis: National Collegiate Athletic Association.

National Collegiate Athletic Association. (2001b). *2000 Divisions II and III graduation-rates report.* Indianapolis: National Collegiate Athletic Association.

National Commission on the Cost of Higher Education (1998). *Straight talk about college costs and prices. Report of the National Commission on the Cost of Higher Education,* Jan. 21, 1998. Washington, DC: Oryx Press.

Nettles, M. T., and Perna, L. W. (1997). *The African American education data book: Higher and adult education* (vol. I). Fairfax, VA: Frederick D. Patterson Research Institute of the College Fund/UNCF.

Neisler, O. J. (1992). Access and retention strategies in higher education: An introductory overview. In M. Lang and C. Ford (Eds.), *Strategies for retaining minority students in higher education.* Springfield: Charles C. Thomas Publisher.

Noel, L., Levitze, R. S., and Saluri, D. (1985). *Increasing student retention.* San Francisco: Jossey-Bass.

Okun, M., Benin, M., and Brandt-Williams, A. (1996). Staying in college: Moderators of the relation between intention and institutional departure. *Journal of Higher Education, 67*(5), 577–596.

Olivas, M. A. (1985). *Latino college students.* New York: Teachers College Press.

Palmer, C. J., Penney, S. W., and Gehring, D. D. (1997). Hate speech and hate crimes: Campus conduct codes and Supreme Court rulings. *NASPA Journal, 34,* 112–122.

Pantages, T. J., and Creedon, C. F. (1978). Studies of college attrition, 1950–1975. *Review of Educational Research, 48*(1), 49–101.

Parker, C. E. (1997). Making retention work. *Black Issues in Higher Education, 13,* 120.

Pascarella, E. (1984). College environmental influences on students' educational aspirations. *Journal of Higher Education, 55*(6), 751–771.

Pascarella, E., and others. (1994). Impacts of on-campus and off-campus work on first-year cognitive outcomes. *Journal of College Student Development, 35*(5), 364–370.

Pascarella, E., and Terenzini, P. (1979). Student-faculty informal contact and college persistence: A further investigation. *Journal of Educational Research, 72*(4), 214–218.

Pascarella, E., and Terenzini, P. (1991). *How college affects students.* San Francisco: Jossey-Bass.

Pavel, D. M., Skinner, R. R., and others (1999, Spring). Native Americans and Alaska Natives in postsecondary education. *Education Statistics Quarterly, 1*(1), 67–74.

Peng, S. S., and Fetters, W. B. (1978). Variables involved in withdrawal during the first two years of college: Preliminary findings from the national longitudinal study of the high school class of 1972. *American Educational Research Journal, 15*(3), 361–372.

Perna, L. W. (1998). The contribution of financial aid to student persistence. *Journal of Student Financial Aid, 28*(3), 25–40.

Perna, L. W. (2000). Differences in the decision to attend college among African Americans, Hispanics, and whites. *Journal of Higher Education, 71*(2), 117–141.

Peterson, S. L. (1993). Career decision-making self-efficacy and institutional integration of underprepared college students. *Research in Higher Education, 34*(6), 659–685.

Pine, J. T. (2001). After affirmative action: Univ. of Calif. alters policies to improve diversity. Retrieved Apr. 2003. [http://www.diversityinc.com/public/1753.cfm].

Porter, O. F. (1989). *Undergraduate completion and persistence at four-year colleges and universities: Completers, persisters, stopouts, and dropouts.* Washington, DC: National Institute of Independent Colleges and Universities.

Quality Education for Minorities. (1990). *Education that works: An action plan for the education of minorities.* Cambridge, MA: Massachusetts Institute of Technology.

Redd, K. E. (2001). *HBCU graduates: Employment, earnings and success after college.* Indianapolis: USA Group Foundation.

Redd, K. E., and Scott, J. A. (1997). AASCU/Sallie Mae National Retention Project, in G. G. Clyburn (ed.) *Policies and practices: A focus on higher education retention* (pp. 7–24). Washington, DC: American Association of State Colleges and Universities.

Reindl, T., and Redd, K. E. (1998). *Institutional aid in the 1990s: The consequences of policy connections.* Washington, DC: American Association of State Colleges and Universities.

Reisberg, L. (2000, April 28). A top university wonders why it has no black freshmen. *Chronicle of Higher Education,* A52–A54.

Rendón, L. I. (1996). Life on the border. *About Campus,* 14–19.

Rendón, L. I. (1997). Access in a democracy: Narrowing the opportunity gap. Unpublished paper presented at the Policy Panel on Access, National Postsecondary Education Cooperative, Sept. 9, 1997.

Rendón, L. I., Jalomo, R., Jr., and Nora, A. (2000). Theoretical considerations in the study of minority student retention in higher education. In J. M. Braxton (Ed.), *Reworking the student departure puzzle* (pp. 127–156). Nashville: Vanderbilt University Press.

Reyes, N. (1997). Holding on to what they've got. *Black Issues in Higher Education, 13,* 36–41.

Richardson, R.C.J., Simmons, H. L., and de los Santos, A.G.J. (1987). Graduating minority students. *Change, 19*(3), 20–27.

Richardson, R.C.J., and Skinner, E. F. (1990). Adapting to diversity: Organizational influences on student achievement. *Journal of Higher Education, 61*(5), 485–511.

Richardson, R.C.J., and Skinner, E. F. (1992, Winter). *Helping first-generation minority students achieve degrees.* New Directions for Community Colleges, no. 80. San Francisco: Jossey-Bass.

Rodarmor, W. (1991, Sept.). California Q&A: A conversation with Troy Duster. *California Monthly.*

Rootman, I. (1972). Voluntary withdrawal from a total adult socializing organization: A model. *Sociology of Education, 45,* 258–270.

Ryan, J. M., and Kuhs, T. M. (1993, Spring). Assessment of preservice teachers and the use of portfolios. *Theory into Practice, 32*(2), 75–81.

St. John, E. P. (1991). What really influences minority attendance? Sequential analysis of the High School and Beyond sophomore cohort. *Research in Higher Education, 32*(2), 141–158.

St. John, E. P. (2001). The impact of aid packages on educational choices: High tuition–high loan and educational opportunity. *Journal of Student Financial Aid, (31)*2: 35–54.

St. John, E. P., Kirshstein, J. R., and Noel, L. (1991). The effects of financial aid on persistence: A sequential analysis. *Review of Higher Education, 14*(3), 383–406.

St. John, E. P., Paulsen, M. B., and Starkey, J. B. (1996). The nexus between college choice and persistence. *Research in Higher Education, 37*(2), 175–220.

St. John, E. P., and Starkey, J. B. (1995). An alternative to net price: Assessing the influence of prices and subsidies on within-year persistence. *Journal of Higher Education, 66*(2), 156–186.

Sallie Mae. (1999). *Supporting the historically black college and university mission: The Sallie Mae/HBCU Default Management Project.* Reston, VA: Sallie Mae.

Sedlacek, W. E., and Prieto, D. O. (1990). Predicting minority students' success in medical school. *Academic Medicine, 65*(3), 161–166.

Selingo, J. (2000). What states aren't saying about the "x-percent solution." *Chronicle of Higher Education.* Retrieved June 2, 2000. [http://www.chronicle.com].

Smedley, B. D., Myers, H. F., and Harrell, S. P. (1993). Minority-status stresses and the college adjustment of ethnic minority freshmen. *Journal of Higher Education, 64*(4), 434–452.

Smith, L., Lippitt, R., and Sprandel, D. (1985). Building support for a campuswide retention program. In L. Noel, R. S. Levitze, D. Saluri, and Associates (Eds.), *Increasing student retention* (pp. 366–382). San Francisco: Jossey-Bass.

Spady, W. G. (1970). Dropouts from higher education: An interdisciplinary review and synthesis. *Interchange, 1*(1), 64–85.

Spady, W. G. (1971). Dropouts from higher education: Toward an empirical model. *Interchange, 2*(3), 38–62.

Spatz, M. A. (1995, Dec. 6). *From high risk to high retention: A look at strategies that transform special admit students into successful collegians.* The Consortium for Student Retention Data Exchange. Retrieved Dec. 18, 2001. [http://www.occe.ou.edu/CSRDE/1995.htm].

Stage, F. K. (1989). Motivation, academic and social integration, and the early dropout. *American Educational Research Journal, 26*(3), 385–402.

Stanley, M. G., and Witten, C. H. (1990). University 101 freshman seminar course: A longitudinal study of persistence, retention, and graduation rates. *NASPA Journal, 27,* 344–352.

Steele, C. (1999). *The compelling need for diversity in higher education.* ERIC document reproduction service no. ED435367.

Steinmiller, R., and Steinmiller, G. (1991). Retention of at-risk students in higher education. In *Reaching our potential: Rural education in the 90s,* conference proceedings, Rural Education Symposium, March 17–20, 1991, Nashville, TN.

Swail, W. S. (1995). *A conceptual framework for student retention in science, engineering, and mathematics.* Dissertation conducted at the George Washington University, Washington, DC.

Swail, W. S. (2000). Preparing America's disadvantaged for college: Programs that increase college opportunity. In A. F. Cabrera and S. M. La Nasa (Eds.), *Understanding the college choice of disadvantaged student* (pp. 85–101). San Francisco: Jossey-Bass.

Swail, W. S., and Perna, L. W. (2002). Pre-college outreach programs: A national perspective. In Tierney and Hagedorn (Eds.), *Increasing access to college.* Albany, NY: State University of New York Press.

Terenzini, P. T., and Pascarella, E. T. (1977). Voluntary freshman attrition and patterns of social and academic integration in a university: A test of a conceptual model. *Research in Higher Education, 6*(1), 25–43.

Terenzini, P. T., and Pascarella, E. T. (1980). Toward the validation of Tinto's model of college student attrition: A review of recent studies. *Research in Higher Education, 12*(3), 271–280.

Terenzini, P. T., and Pascarella, E. T. (1984). Freshman attrition and the residential context. *Review of Higher Education, 7*(2), 111–124.

Terenzini, P. T., and Wright, T. M. (1987). *The influence of academic and social integration on students' personal development during four years of college.* Paper presented at the annual forum of AIR, May 3–6, 1987, Kansas City, MO.

Thayer, P. (2000, May). Retaining first generation and low income students. *Opportunity Outlook,* pp. 2–8.

Thomas, G. E. (1986). *The access and success of blacks and Latinos in U.S. graduate and professional education.* Working paper. Washington, DC: National Research Council.

Tierney, W. G. (1992). An anthropological analysis of student participation in college. *Journal of Higher Education, 63*(6), 603–618.

Tinto, V. (1975). Dropout from higher education: A theoretical synthesis of recent research. *Review of Higher Education, 45*(1), 89–125.

Tinto, V. (1982). Limits of theory and practice in student attrition. *Journal of Higher Education, 53*(6), 687–700.

Tinto, V. (1988). Stages of student departure: Reflections on the longitudinal character of student leaving. *Journal of Higher Education, 59*(4), 438–455.

Tinto, V. (1993). *Leaving college: Rethinking the causes and cures of student attrition* (2nd ed.). Chicago: University of Chicago Press.

Tinto, V. (1997). *From access to participation.* Washington, DC: National Postsecondary Education Cooperative.

Tinto, V. (2000). Linking learning and leaving. In J. M. Braxton (Ed.), *Reworking the student departure puzzle.* Nashville: Vanderbilt University Press.

Tobias, S. (1990). *They're not dumb. They're different.* Tucson, AZ: Research Corporation.

Tracey, T. J., and Sedlacek, W. E. (1985). The relationship of noncognitive variables to academic success: A longitudinal comparison by race. *Journal of College Student Personnel,* 405–410.

Trippi, J., and Cheatham, H. E. (1989). Effects of special counseling programs for black freshmen on a predominately white campus. *Journal of College Student Development, 30,* 144–151.

Ugbah, S., and Williams, S. A. (1989). The mentor-protégé relationship: Its impact on blacks in predominantly white institutions. In J. Elam (Ed.), *Blacks in higher education overcoming the odds* (pp. 29–42). Lanham, MD: University Press of America.

U.S. Census Bureau. (2001). Household income data from current population survey. Retrieved Aug. 13, 2003. [http://www.census.gov/hhes/income/income01/inctab1.html].

U.S. Department of Education. (1996). *National education longitudinal study 1988/94.* Washington, DC: National Center for Education Statistics.

U.S. Department of Education. (1997). *Reading and mathematics achievement: Growth in high school. An issue brief.* Washington, DC: U.S. Department of Education.

U.S. Department of Education. (2001a). *The condition of education.* Washington, DC: National Center for Education Statistics.

U.S. Department of Education. (2001b). *Digest of education statistics, 2000* (Report No. 2001–034). Washington, DC: National Center for Education Statistics.

U.S. Department of Education. (2001c). *2000 national postsecondary student aid study dataset.* Washington, DC: National Center for Education Statistics.

U.S. General Accounting Office. (1995). Higher education: Restructuring student aid could reduce low-income student dropout rate. Report to Congressional Requesters, March 1995. GAO/HEHS-95-48. Washington, DC: U.S. General Accounting Office.

Valentine, C. A. (1971). Deficit, difference, and bicultural models of Afro-American behavior. *Harvard Educational Review, 41*(2), 137–157.

Vernez, G., Krop, R. A., and Rydell, C. P. (1999). *Closing the education gap: Benefits and costs.* Santa Monica, CA: RAND.

Western Interstate Commission for Higher Education. (1998). *Knocking at the college door: Projections of high school graduates by state and race/ethnicity, 1996–2016.* Boulder, CO: Western Interstate Commission for Higher Education.

Whimbey, A., and others. (1980). Teaching critical reading and analytical reasoning in project SOAR. *Journal of Reading, 24*(1), 5–10.

Wilhelm, T. J., and Wallace, K. M. (1997). *Wayne State University undergraduate retention program.* Consortium for Student Retention Data Exchange. Retrieved Dec. 18, 2001. [http://www.occe.ou.edu/CSRDE/1997.htm].

Williams, P. (2003). Gratz v. Michigan: Undergraduate affirmative action program struck down. *MSNBC News Online.* [http://www.msnbc.com/news/893295.asp]. Accessed Oct. 29, 2003.

Wolanin, T. (1998). Pell Grants: A 25-year history. In L. E. Gladieux, B. Astor, and W. S. Swail (Eds.), *Memory, reason, imagination: A quarter century of Pell Grants* (pp. 13–31). New York: College Board.

Young, J. (1999). *The freshman year initiative at Fayetteville State University: A comprehensive approach to student success.* Consortium for Student Retention Data Exchange.

Watson Scott Swail, Ed.D., is president of the Educational Policy Institute, a Washington, D.C.–based nonprofit organization dedicated to policy research on educational opportunity. His most recent publications include "Higher Education and the New Demographics" (*Change,* 2002), "Precollege Outreach Programs: A National Perspective" in Tierney and Hagedorn's *Increasing Access to College,* and "Beyond Access: Increasing the Odds of College Success" *(Phi Delta Kappan,* May 2000). Swail also serves on a number of national advisory committees, including technical review panels for the major U.S. longitudinal and cross-sectional surveys sponsored by the U.S. Department of Education. Swail received his doctorate in educational policy from George Washington University.

Kenneth E. Redd is director of research and policy analysis for the National Association of Student Financial Aid Administrators in Washington, D.C. He provides research and data analysis on numerous issues in higher education, particularly in trends in the financing of undergraduate and graduate education, student enrollments, access, and degree completion. Before joining NASFAA, Redd was director of higher education research for the USA Group Foundation and served in research positions for the National Association for Independent Colleges and Universities and the American Association of State Colleges and Universities. Redd is the author or coauthor of numerous research reports, book chapters, and journal articles on a wide variety of issues in higher education.

Laura W. Perna is an assistant professor in the Department of Education Policy and Leadership at the University of Maryland. Her research focuses on policies and practices related to college access and choice as well as equity in faculty reward systems. Findings of her research have been published in numerous journals and edited books. She has received funding for her research from the Lumina Foundation for Education, the Association for Institutional Research, and the American Educational Research Association.

The Educational Policy Institute, Inc., is a nonprofit, nonpartisan, and nongovernmental organization dedicated to policy-based research on educational opportunity for all students. With offices in Washington, D.C., Los Angeles, and Toronto, EPI is a collective association of researchers and policy analysts from around the world dedicated to the mission of enhancing our knowledge of critical barriers facing students and families throughout the educational pipeline. In addition, EPI has developed extensive partnerships and collaborative arrangements with other leading research and educational organizations, further supporting its mission and ability to conduct policy-relevant research for practical use.

The mission of EPI is to expand educational opportunity for low-income and other historically underrepresented students through high-level research and analysis. By providing educational leaders and policymakers with the information required to make prudent programmatic and policy decisions, the doors of opportunity can be further opened for all students, resulting in an increase in the number of students prepared for, enrolled in, and completing postsecondary education.

For more information about EPI, please visit our Web site, http://www.educationalpolicy.org.

Name Index

A

Abel, R., 159
Adamany, D., 135
Adelman, C., 10, 12, 27, 51, 54–56, 99, 145
Ajzen, I., 48
Alexander, K. L., 12
Allen, D., 44
Alwin, W. F., 12
Amdahl, G., 113
Ancis, J. R., 59
Anderson, B. T., 56
Anderson, E., 50, 75, 76, 78
Arendale, D. R., 150
Arrington, P. G., 60
Astin, A. W., 51, 55, 61–67, 92, 94–96, 109, 113

B

Bakst, D., 34, 35
Ball, S. R., 59, 60
Beal, P. E., 43, 65, 100
Bean, J. P., 7, 8, 46–48, 50, 55, 70, 75, 78, 148
Bean, L., 35
Beil, C., 62, 145, 146
Bell, C., 9
Benin, M., 61, 62
Bennett, C., 59, 146
Bentler, P. M., 448
Berg, J. H., 64
Berkner, L., 12, 13, 18, 20, 26, 27
Berman, D., 139

Berryman, S. E., 55
Birk, N. A., 135
Black, L. C., 0, 59
Blanchette, C. M., 72
Borman, G. D., 51
Bowen, H. R., 28, 30
Bramlett, D., 137
Brandt-Williams, A., 61, 62
Braxton, J. M., 12, 49
Brinkman, P. T., 28
Brower, A. M., 44, 46
Brunner, B., 33, 34
Burkam, K. R., 12
Bush, G. W., 52

C

Cabrera, A. F., 12, 43, 44, 48, 61, 62, 70, 157
Capella, B., 64
Carpenter, L. C., 51
Castaneda, M. B., 43, 44, 48, 61, 62, 70
Cataldi, E. F., 18, 26, 27
Chanault, K., 36
Chavez, L., 12, 13, 18, 20, 26
Chavis, O. D., 136
Cheatham, H. E., 109
Chickering, A. W., 66, 67, 109
Christman, D. E., 68
Clayton, M., r
Clewell, B., 114
Clyde, P., 143
Cohen, R., 35, 36
Collison, M., 94

W

Wallace, D., 159
Wallace, K. M., 135
Watson, M., 141
Whimbey, A., 101
Whitlock, E. R., 46
Wilhem, T. J., 135
Williams, P., 35
Williams, S. A., 35, 65, 100
Witten, C. H., 139

Wolanin, T., 10
Wright, T. M., 63, 64
Wu, Z., 70, 72

Y

Young, J., 136

Z

Zea, M. C., 62

Subject Index

A

AASCU/Sallie Mae National Retention Project, 120, 122

Academic advising, 100–103

Academic preparation, 51–57, 127
  and commitment to educational goals and institution, 61–63
  campus climate and, 57–61
  and course selection and integrity, 55–57
  financial aid and, 67–68
  and National Assessment of Educational Progress (NAEP), 53–54
  recent financial aid policy developments and, 68–70
  SAT comparison and, 52–53
  social and academic integration and, 63–67

Academic services component, 100–103, 101*fig*.25

Access, 9–11

Accessibility, 107, 108

ACT, 52, 132, 149, 150

Advisory Committee on Student Financial Assistance, 68

Affirmative Action
  brief history of, in higher education, 33–34
  and challenges to Bakke standard, 34–36
  direction of, 40–41
  and expanded role for
  minority-serving institutions, 38–40
  in future, 32–33
  and "X percent" solution, 36–38

Affordability, 127

American Council on Education, 69, 70

American River College (Sacramento, CA), 131

Application process, 94

Arizona, 152

Arkansas State University, 143, 144

Assessment methods, alternative, 99, 105

Assessment strategies, 104, 107

Association for Institutional Research, 147

Association for International Research, 149

Association for the Study of Higher Education, 146, 148

Association of Medical Colleges, 55, 56

Attrition theories, 75

B

Bachelor's degree
  and access to advanced degrees and careers, 30–31
  attainment rates, 26–27
  and benefits to society, 29–30
  and differences in economic benefits, 27–29
  and distribution of enrollments and degree recipients by race or ethnicity, 25

Excel Program
  at Wayne State University, 134, 135
  at West Virginia University, 141
Executive Order 10925 (Kennedy), 33

F

Faculty
  development and resources, 104,
    106, 126
  reward systems, 126
  informal contact of, with student
    103, 110
Fayetteville State University
  (Fayetteville, NC), 135
Financial aid, 67–68
  availability of need-based, 95–96
  office, 123, 124
  packaging of, 96
  and persistence, 70–71
  recent policy developments in, 68–70
Financial counseling, 95
First-year Learning Team (FLighT) Program
  (Southeast Missouri State University), 135
Flexible planning, 126
Florida, 2, 35, 37
Force field analysis of college persistence
  (Anderson), 50*fig*.15, 76
Fort Peck Community College
  (Poplar, MT), 123
Free Application for Federal Student Aid
  (FAFSA), 94
Freshman Year Initiative Program
  at Bronx Community College, 138, 139
  at Fayetteville State University, 136
Funding priorities, 126

G

Gatekeeping, 98
  and gatekeeper courses, 56
GEARUP (Gaining Early Awareness and
  Readiness for Undergraduate Programs),
  102
G.I. Bill (Serviceman's Readjustment Act
  of 1944), 9
Glendale Community College
  (Glendale, AZ), 138

Goal commitment, 61, 62, 78
Grade point averages (GPA), 64, 87,
  98, 141
Grants, 95
  versus loans, 71–73
Gratz v. Bollinger, 32
Group collaborative approach, 105–106
Grutter v. *Bollinger,* 32, 33, 38, 39, 41

H

Hands-on approach, 105–106
HBCUs (Historically Black Colleges and
  Universities), 11, 21–24, 32, 33, 38–40,
  58, 59, 64, 66, 148
High School and Beyond database, 55,
  72, 145
Higher Education Act (1965), 2, 9, 10
Hope Scholarship Tax Credit, 69
Hopwood v. Texas, 34, 35
Housing, 108, 110
HSIs (Hispanic-Serving Institutions),
  21, 22, 24, 32, 33, 39, 40

I

Income, median annual household,
  by educational attainment of
    householder, 5
Incorporation stage, 46
Indiana University, 146
Indiana Wesleyan University
  (Marion, IN), 140
Information
  dissemination of, 95
  lack of, 94
Institute for Higher Education Policy, 67
Institutional change, process of, 116
Institutional commitment, 61, 62
Institutional leadership, 125
Instructional practices, 106
Instructional strategies, 104
Integrated Postsecondary Education
  21, 20
Integrated Postsecondary Education Data
  System (IPEDS)
  1997 Fall Staff Survey, 66
  1999 Fall Enrollment Survey, 20

Integration, student. *See* Student integration
Integrity, 55–57

J

Johnson v. Board of Regents of the University of Georgia, 35
Journal of Higher Education, 155
Journal of Psychology, 148

K

Keene State University (Keene, NH), 144

L

Leadership
   importance of, on student retention, 120–125
   institutional, 125
Level playing field, 34
Lewis-Clark State College (Lewiston, ID), 142, 143
Lifetime Learning Tax Credit, 69
Loans, grants *versus,* 71–73
Long Beach City College (Long Beach, CA), 137, 138
Loyola University (New Orleans), 136
Lubin House (Syracuse University), 98

M

Mathematics Workshop Program (University of California–Berkeley), 64–65
Medicaid, 6, 28, 30
Medicare, 6
Mentoring, 101, 102
Merrill Lynch, 36
MESA (Mathematics, Engineering, and Science Achievement), 102
Michigan, 38
Minorities
   and academic preparation for college, 12–13
   and enrollment in college, 15–21
   and graduation from high school, 13–15

   and persistence in college to and bachelor's degree completion, 21
Missouri, 38
Model Institutions for Excellence (MIE) Program (Bowie State University), 142
Morgan State University (Baltimore, MD), 122
Morrill Act (1862), 11
Morrill Act II (1892), 11
MSEN (Mathematics and Science Education Network), 102
Multiculturalism, 109
Multiple intelligence theory (Gardner), 78n3, 87

N

National Aeronautics and Space Administration, 142
National Assessment of Educational Progress (NAEP), 53–55
National Association of State Student Grant and Aid Programs, 41, 52–53
National Association of Student Financial Aid Administrators (ASFAA), 95n7
National Center for Educational Statistics (NCES), 25, 26, 31, 37, 40, 54, 95, 148
National Collegiate Athletic Association (NCAA), 39
National Commission on the Cost of Higher Education, 94n.5
National Educational Longitudinal Study (NELS:1992), 12, 54
National Educational Longitudinal Study (NELS:1988), 18
National Postsecondary Education Cooperative, 10
National Postsecondary Student Aid Study, 148
National Press Club, 8
National Resource Center for the First-Year Experience and Students in Transition, 139
National Science Foundation, 142
Native American Higher Education Consortium, 152

NCES. *See* National Center for Educational Statistics (NCES)
NELS. *See* National Educational Longitudinal Study
New Mexico, 152
Northern Illinois University, 137

O

Office of Retention Programs (Northern Illinois University), 137
Oglala Lakota College (South Dakota), 142
Ohio University at Athens, 65
Oklahoma, 152
"One Florida" plan, 35
Opportunity Outlook, 158
Orientation
  freshman, 99–100
  on-campus living, 99

P

Parental support, 78
Peer support, 78
Pell Grant, 2, 9, 69, 70, 153, 154
Persistence, student. *See* Student persistence
Phi Delta Kappan, 146
Plantation economics, 151
Pluralism, 107
Postsecondary Education Opportunity, 150, 151
Postsecondary opportunity
  and Affirmative Action in America, 31–41
  and education pipeline for racial and ethnic minorities, 11–31
  and growing importance of college degree, 4–9
  and moving from access to success, 9–11
Pre-college programs, 98, 99, 101–103
Preparedness, academic, 51–57
Presidents, 122
Princeton University, 92, 93
Problem-solving ability, 78
Professional development, 106
Project SOAR (Xavier University), 64–65
Proposition 209, 35, 127

Proprietary schools, 10
Psychological model (Bean and Eaton), 46–48, 47*fig*.14
  shortcomings of, 48–50
PWIs (Predominantly White Institutions), 57–61, 64, 66, 148, 152, 155, 156

Q

Quality Education for Minorities, 55

R

Racial minorities, education pipeline for, 11–31
RAND Corporation, 6
Reciprocity, 81
Regents of the University of California v. Bakke, 34–36
Research Assistants (RAs), 101
Research in Higher Education, 154, 157
Research
  institutional, 126
  opportunities, 101, 102
Retention. *See* Student retention; Student retention framework; Student retention program, implementation of
Reverse discrimination, 35
Review of Educational Research, 159
Review of Higher Education, 158
Rigorous coursework, 12*n*1
Risk Point Intervention Program (University of Texas, San Antonio), 133, 134
Role models, 65–66

S

Saint Xavier University (Chicago), 132
Sallie Mae, 40, 120, 122
SAT. *See* Scholastic Aptitude Test
Scheduling, flexible, 109, 110
Scholastic Aptitude Test (SAT), 12, 37, 52, 69, 87, 98, 99
Separation stage, 46
Social anthropology theory, 46, 49, 79
Socioeconomic status, 4, 5
Southeast Missouri State University (Cape Girardeau, MO), 135

About the ASHE-ERIC Higher Education Reports Series

Since 1983, the ASHE-ERIC Higher Education Report Series has been providing researchers, scholars, and practitioners with timely and substantive information on the critical issues facing higher education. Each monograph presents a definitive analysis of a higher education problem or issue, based on a thorough synthesis of significant literature and institutional experiences. Topics range from planning to diversity and multiculturalism, to performance indicators, to curricular innovations. The mission of the Series is to link the best of higher education research and practice to inform decision making and policy. The reports connect conventional wisdom with research and are designed to help busy individuals keep up with the higher education literature. Authors are scholars and practitioners in the academic community. Each report includes an executive summary, review of the pertinent literature, descriptions of effective educational practices, and a summary of key issues to keep in mind to improve educational policies and practice.

The Series is one of the most peer reviewed in higher education. A National Advisory Board made up of ASHE members reviews proposals. A National Review Board of ASHE scholars and practitioners reviews completed manuscripts. Six monographs are published each year and they are approximately 120 pages in length. The reports are widely disseminated through Jossey-Bass and John Wiley & Sons, and they are available online to subscribing institutions through Wiley InterScience (http://www.interscience.wiley.com).

Call for Proposals

The ASHE-ERIC Higher Education Report Series is actively looking for proposals. We encourage you to contact the editor, Dr. Adrianna Kezar, at kezar@usc.edu with your ideas. For detailed information about the Series, please visit http://www.eriche.org/publications/writing.html.

Recent Titles

Back Issue/Subscription Order Form

Copy or detach and send to:
Jossey-Bass, A Wiley Company, 989 Market Street, San Francisco CA 94103-1741

Call or fax toll-free: Phone 888-378-2537 6:30AM – 3PM PST; Fax 888-481-2665

Back Issues: Please send me the following issues at $24 each
(Important: please include series abbreviation and issue number.
For example AEHE28:1)

_____

_____

_____

$ _____   Total for single issues

$ _____   SHIPPING CHARGES: SURFACE   Domestic Canadian
                              First Item $5.00 $6.00
                              Each Add'l Item $3.00 $1.50
                 For next-day and second-day delivery rates, call the number listed above.

Subscriptions   Please ❑ start ❑ renew my subscription to *ASHE-ERIC Higher
                 Education Reports* for the year 2_____at the following rate:

U.S.	❑ Individual $165	❑ Institutional $165
Canada	❑ Individual $165	❑ Institutional $225
All Others	❑ Individual $213	❑ Institutional $276
Online Subscription		❑ Institutional $150

**For more information about online subscriptions visit
www.interscience.wiley.com**

$ _____   Total single issues and subscriptions (Add appropriate sales tax
                 for your state for single issue orders. No sales tax for U.S.
                 subscriptions. Canadian residents, add GST for subscriptions and
                 single issues.)

❑Payment enclosed (U.S. check or money order only)
❑VISA ❑ MC ❑ AmEx _____ Exp. Date _____

Signature _____ Day Phone _____
❑ Bill Me (U.S. institutional orders only. Purchase order required.)

Purchase order # _____
                 Federal Tax ID13559302   **GST 89102 8052**

Name _____

Address _____

_____

Phone _____ E-mail _____

For more information about Jossey-Bass, visit our Web site at www.josseybass.com

PROMOTION CODE ND03

ASHE-ERIC HIGHER EDUCATION REPORT
IS NOW AVAILABLE ONLINE AT WILEY INTERSCIENCE

What is Wiley InterScience?

Wiley InterScience is the dynamic online content service from John Wiley & Sons delivering the full text of over 300 leading scientific, technical, medical, and professional journals, plus major reference works, the acclaimed Current Protocols laboratory manuals, and even the full text of select Wiley print books online.

What are some special features of Wiley InterScience?

Wiley Interscience Alerts is a service that delivers table of contents via e-mail for any journal available on Wiley InterScience as soon as a new issue is published online.
Early View is Wiley's exclusive service presenting individual articles online as soon as they are ready, even before the release of the compiled print issue. These articles are complete, peer-reviewed, and citable.
CrossRef is the innovative multi-publisher reference linking system enabling readers to move seamlessly from a reference in a journal article to the cited publication, typically located on a different server and published by a different publisher.

How can I access Wiley InterScience?

Visit http://www.interscience.wiley.com.

Guest Users can browse Wiley InterScience for unrestricted access to journal Tables of Contents and Article Abstracts, or use the powerful search engine.
Registered Users are provided with a *Personal Home Page* to store and manage customized alerts, searches, and links to favorite journals and articles. Additionally, Registered Users can view free Online Sample Issues and preview selected material from major reference works.
Licensed Customers are entitled to access full-text journal articles in PDF, with select journals also offering full-text HTML.

How do I become an Authorized User?

Authorized Users are individuals authorized by a paying Customer to have access to the journals in Wiley InterScience. For example, a University that subscribes to Wiley journals is considered to be the Customer.
Faculty, staff and students authorized by the University to have access to those journals in Wiley InterScience are Authorized Users. Users should contact their Library for information on which Wiley journals they have access to in Wiley InterScience.

ASK YOUR INSTITUTION ABOUT WILEY INTERSCIENCE TODAY!